VEGETARIAN

THE FOOD LOVER'S GUIDE TO VEGETARIAN COOKING

VEGETARIAN

THE FOOD LOVER'S GUIDE TO VEGETARIAN COOKING

THUNDER BAY
P·R·E·S·S

Published in the United States by
Thunder Bay Press,
An imprint of the Advantage Publishers Group
5880 Oberlin Drive
San Diego, CA 92121-4794
www.advantagebooksonline.com

QUMBCVG

ISBN 1-57145-233-8

Library of Congress Cataloging-in-Publication Data available upon request.

1 2 3 4 5 00 01 02 03 04

This book is produced by
Quantum Books
The Old Brewery, 6 Blundell Street
London N7 9BH

Designer: Bruce Low
Editor: Sarah King

This book was compiled using material from:
Healthy Vegetarian Cooking, Very Vegetarian Cooking, The Hot and Spicy Cookbook, The Vegetarian Cookbook and Herbs, Herbs, Herbs

Manufactured in Singapore by Eray Scan
Printed in Singapore by Star Standard Industries Pte. Ltd.

Contents
....

INTRODUCTION

Vegetarianism is now a way of life for many people all over the world. With vegetarian dishes included on the menu in restaurants, bars, offices, and at special functions etc., vegetarians no longer need to feel like 'special' or 'awkward' cases. The range of vegetarian dishes is so vast, varied and appealing that meat-eaters too are often tempted away from the traditional dishes to the vegetarian option.

The reasons for becoming vegetarian vary. They could stem from a straight forward dislike of the taste of meat, an aversion to killing animals, a desire to find a healthier way of living, or simply a love of fruit, vegetables, grains, pulses, and dairy produce.

Whatever the reason for becoming vegetarian, it is important to appreciate that simply cutting out the meat content of traditional dishes is not going to result in a healthy diet. Children, especially, need a good balance of proteins, carbohydrates, fats, fiber, vitamins, and essential minerals while they are growing and adults, too, should include all these elements in their diet to ensure good health.

Fresh fruit and vegetables are now widely available all year round. Organically grown produce is coming into its own as concern grows amongst consumers about the effects on the environment of the use of fertilizers and genetically modified crops. Organically grown

produce is certainly very tasty and well worth buying if stocked by local supermarkets or stores at affordable prices. Even better, see if there is a local organic farm that sells its produce direct to the consumer.

Herbs and spices are an essential element of many vegetarian recipes, adding flavor and color to the dishes. Most of the recipes in this book recommend using fresh herbs. Home-grown herbs are a good idea if circumstances permit. If you are lucky enough to have your own back yard, turn a corner of it into a herb garden. Alternatively buy some pots and grow your herbs in the kitchen. If dried herbs are used instead, then the quantities should be reduced. As a general rule, substitute 1 teaspoon of dried herbs for 1 tablespoon of fresh ones.

Pulses and grains are a popular element of the vegetarian diet and are extremely tasty. Sometimes preparation in advance is needed so check to see whether beans and peas etc. will need soaking overnight. It is essential that instructions are followed closely as the soaking of beans and peas is done to remove harmful toxins. Always check the instructions on the packet or can.

Dairy produce is also a good source of protein and there are plenty of delicious cheeses available nowadays. Try experimenting with different types and see how they can change the flavor of a favorite recipe. Do not, however, overdo the cosumption of dairy proucts believing that they are the only foods that contain the protein that you may be lacking as a result of following a meat-free diet. A dairy-rich diet could increase your cholesterol to an unhealthy level.

Remember that other foods, such as soya, tofu, and nuts contain protein too.

There are now plenty of 'meat substitutes' on the market which look and taste very similar to the real thing. Whether you miss meat or not, these substitutes (such as tofu in a stir-fry) can make a very pleasant and nutritious addition to a vegetarian meal.

Vegetarian cooking does not require any special equipment, although

crispness and a blender is an essential item for making vegetable soups.

This book contains tasty vegetarian dishes from all over the world. For ease of reference it is divided into: soups and starters; main dishes; pasta; side dishes and salads; and desserts.

you will find a wok and a blender invaluable investments. Wok-fried vegetables retain their flavor and

OVEN TEMPERATURES GUIDE		
C	F	Gas Mark
240	475	9
230	450	8
220	425	7
200	400	6
190	375	5
180	350	4
165	325	3
150	300	2
140	275	1
125	250	$^1/_2$
110	225	$^1/_4$

Chapter One

Soups and Starters

A selection of mouthwatering soups and hors d'oeuvres to wet your appetite. Many of these starters can be adapted to form the main or side dish.

BORSCHT

SERVES 6

INGREDIENTS

2 large onions

3 large beets

3 large carrots

2 parsnips

4 stalks celery

3 Tbsp tomato paste

4 large tomatoes

½ small white cabbage, shredded

1 Tbsp honey

1 Tbsp lemon juice

salt and freshly ground black pepper

handful of chopped parsley

all-purpose white flour

low-fat sour cream or yogurt

Quintessentially Russian, borsch is a fresh-tasting, healthy soup which can be served hot or cold depending on the occasion. Beet is a naturally sweet vegetable, and gives the soup a unique flavour.

Cut onions, beet, carrots, parsnips, and celery into matchsticks. Bring a large pan of salted water to a boil, add the tomato paste and the vegetables and simmer for 30 minutes until tender.

Skin the tomatoes, remove the seeds, and chop. Add to the pan with the cabbage, honey, lemon juice, and seasoning. Simmer for 5 minutes, then throw in a handful of chopped parsley. Check seasoning.

If necessary, thicken the soup with a blend of little flour and low-fat sour cream. The soup is best made the day before it is to be eaten. Reheat and serve with a bowl of low-fat sour cream or yogurt.

CREAMY GARLIC MUSHROOMS

SERVES 4

INGREDIENTS

2 Tbsp olive oil

1 large garlic clove, crushed

2 scallions, chopped

salt and freshly ground black pepper

300 g/12 oz button mushrooms

150 g/6 oz low-fat soft cheese

a little parsley, chopped (optional)

These are perfect baked-potato fillers!

Heat the oil in a large skillet. Add the garlic, scallions, and seasoning, and cook for 2 minutes. Then add all the mushrooms and toss them over high heat for a couple of minutes, until they are hot. Do not cook the mushroom until their juices run as they will be too watery.

AVOCADO AND POMEGRANATE SALAD

SERVES 4

INGREDIENTS

1 ripe pomegranate, cut in half

1 cup black grapes, cut in half and seeded

2 small ripe avocados

1 tbsp lemon juice

Dressing

4 tbsp white-wine vinegar

2 tbsp orange juice

salt and freshly ground black pepper

1 tsp honey

1 tsp olive oil

1 tbsp peanut or sunflower oil

2 tbsp chopped fresh mint

Garnish

fresh mint leaves

In a small bowl, whisk together wine vinegar, orange juice, salt and pepper to taste and honey. Slowly whisk in olive oil and vegetable oil until dressing is thick and creamy. Stir in the chopped mint. Set aside.

Into a medium bowl, scrape seeds out of pomegranate halves. Add grape halves and toss to mix.

Cut avocados in half and remove pits. Using a round-bladed knife, run it between skin and flesh of avocados, working skin away from flesh until skin is removed.

Place avocados, round-side up, on work surface and, using a sharp knife and starting ½ inch below stem end, cut avocado lengthwise into ¼-inch slices, leaving stem end intact. Arrange each sliced avocado half on 4 individual plates. Using palm of hand, gently push avocado slices forward to fan out slices. Sprinkle lemon juice over them.

Sprinkle a quarter of the pomegranate seed-grape mixture on to each avocado half and spoon over dressing. Garnish each plate with a few mint leaves.

ONION, LENTIL, AND LEMON SOUP

SERVES 4

INGREDIENTS

1 cup/200 ml/7 floz water

⅓ cup plus 1 Tbsp pearl barley

1 Tbsp tomato paste

6¼ cups/1.5 1/2½ pt vegetable stock

¾ cup/175 g/6 oz lentils, rinsed and picked over

5 onions, sliced very thinly

1 tsp dried anise seeds

juice of 1 large lemon

large pinch of sweet paprika

pinch of cayenne pepper

salt and freshly ground black pepper

Garnish

12 paper-thin lemon slices

Barley and lentils are two Armenian favourites paired in this earthy soup. Served with warm cornbread, it would make a filling supper or lunch.

Bring the water to a boil in a large enamelled or stainless steel saucepan. Stir in the barley, cover, and simmer over low heat for about 20–25 minutes, until the barley is just tender and the water has been absorbed. Stir in the tomato paste, vegetable stock, lentils, onions, and anise. Bring to the boil, cover, and simmer over low heat for 1 hour, or until the lentils are soft.

Stir in the lemon juice, paprika, cayenne pepper, and salt and pepper to taste, and simmer uncovered for a further 20 minutes. Pour the soup into heated bowls, and garnish each with two very thin slices of lemon.

TOMATO AND CILANTRO SOUP

SERVES 6

This is a refreshing cold summer soup that would make an excellent first course to a fish or poultry main dish. The citrus-like flavor of the cilantro perfectly complements the fruit juices in this refreshing soup.

In a blender or food processor fitted with a metal blade, purée the tomatoes, onion, tomato juice, orange juice, red bell pepper and sugar.

Press the purée through a strainer, rubbing with a wooden spoon to force as much through as possible. Discard the residue, and add sufficient iced water to thin the purée to a soup-like consistency. Stir in the cilantro, cover, and chill. Pass the yogurt at the table, to allow guests to add as much as they wish.

INGREDIENTS

1.3 kg/3 lb ripe, plump tomatoes, roughly chopped

1 small onion, chopped

2½ cups/1.5 l/2½ pt tomato juice

3 Tbsp freshly squeezed orange juice

1 Greek or Italian pickled red pepper, seeded

¼ tsp caster sugar

iced water

4 Tbsp finely chopped fresh cilantro

Greek yogurt, to serve

INGREDIENTS

4 large ripe tomatoes, sliced
bunch of fresh basil
4–6 thin slices of red onion
salt to taste
freshly, ground black pepper
low-fat mozzarella-type cheese

TOMATO AND BASIL SALAD

SERVES 4

Take advantage of the ripe tomatoes and surplus of basil from summer gardens with this cool and elegant – but simple salad. Drizzle your favorite low-fat dressing on top.

Slice the tomatoes, salt lightly, and let them drain on paper towels for about 20 minutes.

Wash the basil and dry well with paper towels or in a salad spinner. Tear the leaves from the stems and arrange a thin layer of leaves on a platter. Top with about half the tomato slices. Separate the onion rings and scatter about half over the tomatoes. Add another layer of basil, tomatoes and onions. Sprinkle lightly with freshly ground black pepper, and garnish with a few extra basil leaves.

A variation is to top the tomatoes with thin slices of the low-fat mozzarella-type cheese.

INGREDIENTS

20 cm/8 inch piece of cucumber, cut in half
lengthwise
½ cup/100 g/4 oz pine nuts toasted
½ cup/220 g/8 oz cottage cheese
4 medium tomatoes, skinned, seeded, and
chopped
2 tsp chopped, fresh dill
1 tsp chopped, frersh mint

Garnish

lettuce leaves
dill sprigs

Do not mix the filling more than a few
minutes before serving, or the nuts will
become soggy and lose their crispness.

NUTTY CUCUMBER BOATS

SERVES 4

*A perfect first course for a hot summer
day, or for an outdoor meal. You could
add texture and flavor – fiber too – by
mixing 2 tablespoons of seedless raisins
into the filling.*

Scoop out the centres of the cucumber
pieces and cut into 2 inch pieces.

A few minutes before serving, mix
together the nuts, cheese, tomatoes, dill
and mint. Spoon into each cucumber
wedge.

Arrange the cucumber "boats" on a
bed of lettuce leaves, garnish with dill
sprigs, and serve at once.

Onion Bhajis

MAKES 10-12

Heat the oil and fry the spices for a minute. Add the onion, and stir until well coated.

Turn down the heat, cover and cook until the onion is tender but not mushy. Leave to cool.

Add salt, egg and gram (garbanzo bean) flour and stir well.

Fry generous half-tablespoonfuls of the mixture in 1 cm/½ inch hot oil, turning them almost immediately. As soon as they are puffy and brown remove them with a slotted spoon and drain on paper towels. Serve warm.

Onion bhajis can be kept warm in a moderate oven for 20 minutes or so before serving, but they cannot be made in advance and reheated.

VARIATION
Make the bhajis half-size and serve with toothpicks.

INGREDIENTS

2 Tbsp oil

½ tsp ground mustard seed

1 tsp fenugreek seed

1 tsp ground turmeric

1 medium onion, minced

pinch chili (chili) powder (optional)

½ tsp salt

1 egg

100 g/4 oz gram (garbanzo bean) flour

oil for frying

INGREDIENTS

450 g/1 lb parsnips

50 g/2 oz butter

1½ tsp ground cilantro

1 tsp ground cumin

½ tsp ground turmeric

Approx. 2 ½ cups/1.5 l milk and broth or
water, mixed

few drops Tabasco

salt and white pepper to taste

2 Tbsp light cream

chopped fresh cilantro or parsley

CURRIED PARSNIP SOUP

SERVES 3 – 4

Scrub and trim the parsnips and chop into ¾ inch dice. Cover with cold water until needed.

Melt the butter in a heavy saucepan and fry the spices in it, without browning, to release the flavors.

Add the drained parsnips and turn until well coated. Add the milk and broth or water and simmer, covered, for 20 minutes or so, until the parsnips are just tender.

Strain, liquidize or process the soup: it should not be absolutely smooth.

Reheat and season to taste with Tabasco, salt and white pepper.

Serve with a swirl of cream in each bowl, together with a sprinkling of fresh cilantro or parsley.

Curried croûtons are also good with this.

INGREDIENTS

3 tamarillos

shredded lettuce

1 cup soft cheese with herbs and garlic

6 Tbsp Greek yogurt or soured cream

1 tsp superfine sugar

3 scallions, chopped

2 large ripe avocados

TAMARILLO AND AVOCADO COCKTAIL

SERVES 4

An excellent appetizer, with an interesting blend of flavors. The egg-shaped tamarillo fruit is native to South America and is also known as a "tree tomato". It has a tough, bitter skin that needs to be peeled, and reveals tart golden pink flesh that is purple-tinged around the seeds.

Peel the tamarillos thinly, halve them lengthwise, and slice across. Arrange a little shredded lettuce on 4 individual plates.

Mix the cheese with the yogurt or sour cream in a bowl. Sprinkle the caster sugar over the tamarillos, mix in the chopped scallions, and leave to stand for 15 minutes.

Quarter and peel the avocados and slice them across.

Arrange the avocado slices on the lettuce, top with the tamarillo mixture, and spoon the cheese and yogurt dressing over the top.

Cheese Bell Peppers

SERVES 4

This is a simple but attractive idea. A slice from each of the red and green bell peppers make a colorful appetizer.

Heat a non-stick frying pan over medium heat until evenly hot, then add the nuts, and cook until browned on all sides. Scatter some salt and cayenne pepper over some paper towels, add the hot nuts, and toss in the seasonings. Chop the nuts roughly when cooled.

Beat the cream cheese until smooth, then add the garlic and nuts. Season to taste with extra salt, if necessary, and black pepper. Cut the tops from the peppers and remove the seeds and cores. Pack the filling into the peppers, pressing it down firmly with the back of a spoon.

Chill the peppers for 2 to 3 hours before slicing. Serve one slice of each colored pepper to each person, with wholewheat toast.

INGREDIENTS

1½ cups/300 g/12 oz mixed shelled nuts (peanuts, cashews, almonds, etc.)

salt

cayenne pepper

2 cups/200 g/8 oz low-fat cream cheese

1 clove garlic, minced

freshly ground black pepper

1 medium red bell pepper

1 medium green bell pepper

wholewheat toast, to serve

GUACAMOLE

SERVES 4

Halve the avocados and scoop out the flesh. Combine in a mortar, blender or food processor with the rest of the ingredients and reduce to a smooth paste, adding a little water if the mixture seems too thick. Chill.

Serve as a dip with corn chips, warmed pita bread or crisp raw vegetables cut into bite-sized chunks.

NOTE
Guacamole will discolor if not eaten soon after it is made. It can, however, be kept in the refrigerator for up to 2 hours if sprinkled with lemon juice and covered with plastic wrap actually touching the surface.

INGREDIENTS

2 ripe avocado pears
1 small onion, roughly chopped or shredded
1 tomato, peeled, seeded and minced
1 clove garlic, crushed
½–1½ fresh green chilies, seeded and chopped
1 Tbsp lime or lemon juice
good pinch salt

BAKED TOMATOES

MAKES 4 LARGE OR 8 SMALL SERVINGS

Baked tomatoes are often regarded as a garnish rather than a serious vegetable dish. Here are some tips for making memorable baked tomatoes: Use tomatoes that are firm, not over-ripe. Time the cooking so you are ready to eat the tomatoes as soon as they come out of the oven. Make your own crisp breadcrumbs by toasting good bread, and grinding it coarsely, rather than using bland, commercial breadcrumbs.

Preheat the oven to 220°C/425°F. Lightly grease a shallow baking pan. Core the tomatoes and cut them in half. Lightly salt the cut sides, and turn the tomatoes cut side down on paper towels to drain while you prepare the topping.

Heat the oil in a small pan. Add the garlic and sauté for 1 to 2 minutes, stirring and watching carefully so it doesn't scorch. If the oil is very hot, you may want to remove the pan from the burner. Add the breadcrumbs, return pan to the heat, and cook for 2 minutes, stirring almost constantly. Add the herbs and onion, continue cooking for about 30 seconds, and remove the pan from the heat. Stir in the Parmesan cheese.

Place the tomatoes, cut side up, on the baking pan. Divide the topping among the tomatoes. Bake until the tomatoes lose their firmness but are not mushy, 15 to 20 minutes. Serve.

INGREDIENTS

4 large tomatoes, firm but ripe

salt

2 Tbsp olive oil

3 garlic cloves, minced

½ cup/100 g/4 oz dried breadcrumbs

2 Tbsp chopped fresh basil or 2 tsp dried

1 minced onion

50 g/2 oz grated Parmesan cheese

MELON SOUP

SERVES 6

2 large Ogen melons, peeled, seeded and chopped

4 Tbsp lime juice

¼ cup/50 g/2 oz superfine sugar

2 large cantaloupe melons, peeled, seeded and chopped

4 Tbsp lemon juice

6 Tbsp natural Greek yogurt

Garnish

ground cinnamon and mint leaves

This ingenious two-tone cold soup – one half of each serving is yellow-orange, the other light green – is a great way of using over-ripe fruit.

In the bowl of a blender or food processor fitted with a metal blade, purée the Ogen melon, lime juice and 2 tablespoons sugar until smooth. Pour the mixture into a jug, cover and chill in the refrigerator .

Rinse out the bowl of the blender or processor and fill with the cantaloupe melon, lemon juice and remaining sugar. Purée until smooth. Pour into a jug, cover and chill in the refrigerator.

When ready to serve, position each soup bowl in front of you. Pick up both jugs, and pour the two soups into a bowl at the same time, one on each side. Repeat with the remaining bowls.

Each soup will be two-tone; use a spoon to gently feather the edges to obtain a softer effect. Top each serving with a spoonful of yogurt. Sprinkle the yogurt with a little cinnamon and garnish with mint leaves. Serve immediately.

INGREDIENTS

1¾ cups/420 ml/14 floz vegetable broth

1 cup/200 g/7 oz dried pasta (any shape)

dash of olive oil

2 carrots, thinly sliced

220 g/8 oz frozen green peas

6 Tbsp chopped fresh cilantro

salt and freshly ground black pepper

shredded cheese, to serve (optional)

VEGETABLE AND CILANTRO SOUP

SERVES 4–6

A light, fresh tasting soup that is ideal as an appetizer, a light lunch or late supper dish.

Bring the vegetable broth to a boil in a large saucepan, and add the pasta with a dash of olive oil. Cook for about 5 minutes, stirring occasionally, then add the sliced carrots. Continue to cook for another 5 minutes, then add the peas and chopped cilantro. Season with salt and black pepper and simmer gently for about 10 minutes, stirring occasionally, until the pasta and carrots are tender. Serve the soup with shredded cheese, sprinkled over the top.

VEGETABLE MEDLEY À LA GRECQUE

SERVES 4

The joy of a dish like this one – a medley of vegetables simmered in a spicy sauce – is that you can use any seasonal produce and blend small quantities of more expensive types with plentiful, inexpensive ones.

Put all the sauce ingredients into a pan, bring to a boil, cover and simmer for 20 minutes, until the liquid has reduced and slightly thickened.

Add the celery, carrots, snowpeasand onions, bring the sauce to a boil. Cover the pan and simmer for 10 minutes or until the vegetables are tender. Remove the bay leaf and stir in half the chopped herbs.

Serve warm as an accompaniment to a main dish, or warm or cold as a first course. Sprinkle with the remaining herb sbefore serving.

INGREDIENTS

2 small celery hearts, outer stalks removed, cut into 1inch slices
12 oz carrots, scraped and cut into julienne strips
1 cup/220 g/8 oz snowpeas, trimmed
100 g/4 oz small onions or shallots, peeled and left whole
2 Tbsp chopped fresh cilantro or mint

Sauce

4 Tbsp tomato paste
1 cup/200 ml/7 floz dry cider
1 cup/200 ml/7 floz water
2 cloves garlic, minced
1 Tbsp sunflower oil
1 tsp mustard seed, lightly crushed
salt and freshly ground black pepper
1 bay leaf

INGREDIENTS

1 large eggplant

4 long scallions, quartered

2 plum tomatoes, quartered

1 Tbsp olive oil

salt and freshly ground black pepper

Dressing

3 Tbsp olive oil

juice of ½ lemon

1 tbsp chopped fresh oregano

MEDITERRANEAN SALSA

SERVES 4

Serve this salsa warm as part of a meal, or toss it into a pan of freshly cooked pasta.

Preheat the broiler to high. Slice the aubergine into 1 cm/½ inch rounds and place on a foil-lined broiler pan with the scallions and tomatoes. Brush with olive oil and sprinkle lightly with salt.

Place the vegetables under the broiler for 8–10 minutes, turning once, until tender and lightly charred. Cut the eggplant slices into cubes and place in a large bowl with the scallions and tomatoes.

Quickly whisk together the dressing ingredients and pour over the warm vegetables. Toss well together and season to taste.

MUSHROOM AND PINE NUT DIP

MAKES ABOUT 250 ml (¹/₂ pt)

Use large, open mushrooms because they have a stronger flavor than the small button variety.

Heat the oil in a saucepan and sauté the finely chopped mushrooms. Cook for about 10 minutes over a moderate heat so that the juices released from the mushrooms evaporate and only the olive oil and concentrated cooked mushrooms are left in the pan. Stir occasionally. Then leave the mixture in the pan to cool.

Meanwhile, place the pine nuts in a single layer on a heatproof baking sheet and place under a hot, preheated broiler.

Broil for 1–2 minutes, turning occasionally, until the pine nuts turn a pale golden color. Remove from the heat and allow to cool.

Place the mushrooms and any olive oil from the pan, the tomatoes, and all but 1 tablespoon of pine nuts in a blender or food processor. Process the mixture for a few seconds until smooth. Transfer to a bowl and season. Cover and chill.

Spoon the dip into a serving bowl and sprinkle with the reserved pine nuts and chopped parsley. Serve with a selection of crackers and crusty bread.

INGREDIENTS

4 Tbsp olive oil

220 g/8 oz large open mushrooms, finely chopped

½ cup/100 g/4 oz pine nuts

200 g/7 oz canned tomatoes, drained and chopped

freshly ground black pepper

1 Tbsp chopped fresh parsley for garnish

crackers and crusty bread, to serve

Garnish

1 Tbsp chopped fresh parsley

GARBANZO BEAN SPREAD

MAKES ABOUT 450 ml (³/₄ pt)

A light and spicy version of the very popular Lebanese appetizer, hummus. Spread on warmed pita bread, the citrus tang comes to the fore.

In the bowl of a blender or food processor fitted with a metal blade, combine the garbanzo beans, garlic and olive oil. Process until almost smooth, stopping to push down the paste from the sides of the bowl; then add the sunflower oil, lemon juice, seasoning to taste, spices and parsley. Process until very smooth, adding a little water if you wish a thinner consistency. Scrape into a bowl and swirl the mixture decoratively.

If desired, before serving, make a small well in the center of the spread and mound in the cinnamon-fried meat. Serve with Arab bread or pita.

INGREDIENTS

375 g/14 oz can garbanzo beans in brine, rinsed and drained
2 garlic cloves, crushed
2 Tbsp olive oil
1 Tbsp sunflower oil
3 Tbsp freshly squeezed lemon juice
salt and freshly ground black pepper
½ tsp cayenne pepper
¼ tsp chili powder
2 Tbsp chopped fresh parsley
220 g/8 oz ground lamb or beef, fried with a little salt, pepper and cinnamon (optional)
Arab bread or pita, to serve

45

INGREDIENTS

1 small, ripe pineapple
1 cup/220 g/8 oz cream cheese
1 Tbsp natural yogurt
1 Tbsp chopped fresh chives
pinch of paprika
freshly ground black pepper
chopped fresh chives for garnish

Garnish

chopped fresh chives
crackers, and strips of celery, cucumber and
carrot, to serve

PINEAPPLE AND CHIVE CHEESE DIP

It is best to serve this dip fairly soon after making; on standing, the fresh pineapple exudes juice that can make the dip too moist.

Cut the pineapple in half lengthwise. Use a sharp knife to carefully cut around the inner edge of the pineapple halves. Scoop out the flesh with a spoon. Place the empty pineapple halves upside down on a deep plate to allow excess juice to run out. Cover and chill in the refrigerator.

Place the pieces in a non-metallic sieve over a bowl and allow any excess juice to drain.

Combine the cottage cheese with the yogurt in a bowl. Stir in the pineapple chunks, chives and paprika. Season to taste with black pepper. Cover and chill.

Just before serving, spoon the dip into the pineapple halves and garnish with chopped chives. Serve with a selection of crackers, and chilled strips of celery, cucumber and carrot.

Chapter Two

Main Dishes

Ideas for family meals or
special dinner party dishes. A
variety of delicious recipes for
the main meal of the day.

FRIED GARLIC AND GARBANZO BEAN SALAD

SERVES 4 – 6

Serve with a selection of salads as part of a meal, or toss with a little Greek yogurt and eat with pita bread for a delicious light lunch.

Heat the oil in a small frying pan and gently cook the garlic cloves and cumin seeds for 5 minutes or so, stirring occasionally, until the garlic is softened but not colored.

Place the garbanzo beans in a serving dish, stir in the fried garlic mixture, mint, cilantro and lime juice. Season to taste and serve while still warm, with Greek yogurt.

INGREDIENTS

2 Tbsp vegetable oil

2 garlic cloves, thinly sliced

1 tsp cumin seeds

275 g/10 oz can garbanzo beans, drained and rinsed

2 Tbsp chopped fresh mint

2 Tbsp chopped fresh cilantro

juice of 1 lime

salt and freshly ground black pepper

Greek yogurt

INGREDIENTS

2 cups/450 g/1 lb dried pasta shapes

dash of olive oil

220 g/8 oz cup mushrooms, quartered

1 red bell pepper, cored, seeded and cut into squares

1 yellow bell pepper, cored, seeded and cut into squares

1½ cups/220 g/8 oz pitted black olives

4 Tbsp fresh basil, minced

2 Tbsp fresh parsley, minced

Dressing

2 tsp red wine vinegar

1 tsp salt

freshly ground black pepper

4 Tbsp extra virgin olive oil

1 garlic clove, minced

1–2 tsp Dijon-style mustard

MUSHROOM AND HERB PASTA SALAD

SERVES 4–8

Any small pasta shapes can be used in this dish. It can be served as a main course for a luncheon, or as a side dish for cold meats.

Bring a large saucepan of water to a boil, and add the pasta and a dash of olive oil. Cook for about 10 minutes, until tender. Drain, and rinse under cold running water. Drain well again.

Place the cooked pasta in a large salad bowl, and add the remaining ingredients. Toss together to combine.

To make the dressing, place all the ingredients in a bottle and shake well. Pour the dressing over the salad and toss together. Cover and refrigerate for at least 30 minutes, then toss again before serving.

CAPONATA RICE SALAD

SERVES 4–6

This recipe combines caponata, a popular relish in Italian cuisine, with Italian arborio, or risotto, rice. Though arborio is preferred, it can be substituted with long grain white rice.

Bring 6 cups/1.7 l/3 pt of water to a boil in a large saucepan. Stir in the salt. Add the rice and cook, uncovered, over a moderate heat for about 12 minutes, until *al dente*. Drain the rice, then rinse it under cold running water, and drain again. Set aside.

While the rice is cooking, sauté the onion with 2 tablespoons of the oil in a skillet over a moderately high heat. Cook for about 5 minutes, until the onion becomes soft and translucent. Add the eggplant, garlic and another tablespoon of the oil, and cook for about 7 minutes, until the eggplant is soft.

Transfer the cooked rice to a large bowl and toss with the remaining olive oil and the balsamic vinegar. Add the cooked eggplant mixture, diced tomatoes, capers, olives and fresh herbs of your choice, tossing to mix well together. Season to taste, and let the salad stand for at least 20 minutes before serving.

INGREDIENTS

1 Tbsp salt

2 cups/450 g/1 lb arborio rice

1 medium onion, cut into small dice

6 Tbsp olive oil

1 small eggplant, diced

2 garlic cloves, minced

3 Tbsp balsamic vinegar

3 large ripe tomatoes, seeded and diced

2 Tbsp drained capers

10 small chopped, pitted green olives

4 Tbsp minced mixed fresh herbs (basil, marjoram, mint, oregano and parsley)

salt and freshly ground black pepper

INGREDIENTS

1¾ cups/300 g/12 oz dried bucatini (long hollow pasta tubes)

dash of olive oil

2 garlic cloves, crushed

1 onion, minced

450 g/1 lb carton puréed tomatoes

4 Tbsp chopped fresh basil

salt and freshly ground black pepper

butter

75 g/3 oz freshly shredded Pecorino or Parmesan cheese

BUCATINI WITH TOMATOES

SERVES 4

When you serve this dish, do not be surprised when your guests ask for second servings. Though it is very filling, the temptation to have more is hard to resist.

Bring a large saucepan of water to the boil, and add the bucatini with the olive oil. Cook for about 10 minutes, stirring occasionally, until tender. Drain and set aside.

Preheat the oven to 200°C/400°F. Place the garlic, onion, tomatoes, fresh basil and seasoning in a large frying pan, and heat until simmering. Cook for about 5 minutes, then remove from the heat.

Grease a shallow ovenproof dish with butter, and arrange the bucatini on top. Curl it around to fit the dish, until it is tightly packed with the pasta.

Spoon the tomato mixture over the top, prodding the pasta to ensure the sauce sinks to the bottom of the dish. Sprinkle with cheese, and bake for 25–30 minutes, until crisp and golden. Cut in to wedges to serve.

INGREDIENTS

450 g/1 lb potatoes, sliced thin

2 garlic cloves, minced

½ cup shredded cheese

1 onion, halved and sliced

2 Tbsp chopped fresh parsley

½ cup/100 ml/4 floz half-fat cream substitute

½ cup/100 ml/4 floz skim milk

ground black pepper

chopped fresh parsley, to garnish

POTATO AND CHEESE LAYER

SERVES 4

This recipe uses half-fat cream substitute in place of full-fat cream. If preferred, substitute with skim milk or vegetable broth.

Cook the potatoes in boiling water for 10 minutes. Drain well. Arrange a layer of potatoes in the base of a shallow oven-proof dish. Add a little garlic, cheese, onion, and parsley. Repeat the layers until all the potatoes, onion, cheese, garlic, and parsley are used, finishing with a layer of cheese.

Mix together the half-fat cream substitute and milk. Season and pour over the potato layers. Bake in the oven at 165°C/325°F for 1½ hours until cooked through and golden brown. Sprinkle with black pepper, garnish with parsley, and serve.

INGREDIENTS

550 g/1¼ lb well-flavoured tomatoes, sliced
¼ cup/100 g/4 oz sheep's cheese (Manchego
or Cabrales), coarsely chopped or sliced
chopped fresh cilantro
olive oil, 4 lemon halves, and salt and pepper,
to serve

TOMATO AND CHEESE SALAD
SERVES 4

The slight tang of a semi-hard sheep's cheese makes an interesting contrast to the cool, sweet and juicy tomatoes. The chopped cilantro complements both flavors to make one of the best tomato-based salads around.

Arrange the tomato slices in a shallow bowl and scatter the cheese on top. Sprinkle with cilantro. Serve with oil, lemon halves and seasoning for each person to add, in that order.

TUNISIAN-STYLE VEGETABLE COUSCOUS

SERVES 4

A prominent feature of North African cooking, couscous is made from particles of hard durum wheat semolina. To pre-cook couscous grains, wash them thoroughly and steam uncovered over a bowl of fast-boiling water for 30 minutes. Spread the couscous on a plate, and sprinkle with cold water before continuing to cook it in this Tunisian-style recipe.

Place the drained garbanzo beans and adzuki beans in separate saucepans, cover with water, and boil rapidly for 10 minutes. Cover and simmer for 30–40 minutes.

Place the garlic, leeks, carrots, cauliflower, zucchini, parsnip, tomato paste, cilantro, turmeric and herbs in a large saucepan. Add water, bring to the boil, then cover and simmer for 20 minutes.

Add the garbanzo beans, adzuki beans, green bell pepper, and tomatoes to the vegetables. Return to the boil.

Place the partly-cooked couscous in a steamer lined with a double thickness of cheesecloth, or a clean tea towel and place over the pan of vegetables. Cover and cook for 15 minutes, stirring the grains once or twice.

Stir the low-fat yogurt into the couscous, and put in a heated serving dish. Season and garnish the vegetables and serve them in another heated dish.

INGREDIENTS

1 cup/220 g/8 oz garbanzo beans, soaked overnight and drained
1 cup/220 g/8 oz adzuki beans, soaked overnight and drained
2 cloves garlic, crushed
2 leeks, sliced
2 carrots, thinly sliced
300 g/12 oz cauliflower florets
3 zucchini, sliced
1 parsnip, thinly sliced
2 Tbsp tomato paste
2 tsp ground cilantro
½ tsp ground turmeric
1 tsp mixed dry herbs
2½ cups/1.5 1/2½ pt water
1 green bell pepper, seeded, cored and sliced
300 g/12 oz tomatoes, skinned and quartered
100 g/4 oz dry grains (to yield 220 g/8 oz) pre-cooked couscous.
2 Tbsp low-fat yogurt
salt and paprika

Garnish

fresh parsley

INGREDIENTS

75 g/3 oz button mushrooms, sliced

2 Tbsp butter

2 celery stalks, sliced

1 clove garlic, crushed

1 medium onion, shredded

1 tbsp wholewheat flour

350 g/4 oz can chopped tomatoes

2½ cups/650 g/1½ lb wholemeal breadcrumbs

1 cup ground walnuts

1 egg

1 tsp dried basil

1 tsp dried oregano

1 Tbsp chopped fresh parsley

salt and freshly ground black bell pepper

100 g/4 oz broccoli spears, cooked

Sauce

2 oz mushrooms, chopped

1 tbsp wholewheatl flour

½ cup/100 ml/3 floz vegetable stock

½ cup/100 ml/3 floz skimmed milk

Garnish

celery leaves

MUSHROOM AND BROCCOLI NUT LOAF

SERVES 4

With its colorful layer of broccoli spears, this vegetarian loaf is both attractive and appetizing. It is equally good served hot or cold, and freezes well.

Prehaeat the oven to 180°C/350°F. Sauté the mushrooms in a saucepan with half of the butter. Drain the slices, and place them in a line down the centre of a lightly greased loaf tin.

Cook the celery, garlic and onion in the same saucepan until softened. Stir in the flour and tomatoes (with juice), and cook until the mixture thickens. Add the breadcrumbs, nuts, egg, herbs and seasoning, and remove from the heat. Spread half of the mixture in the loaf tin. Add the broccoli spears, and top with the remaining mixture.

Cover the pan with aluminum foil, place it in a roasting tin half-filled with boiling water, and bake in the oven for 1¼–1½ hours.

For the sauce, melt the remaining butter, add the chopped mushrooms, and cook for 2–3 minutes. Stir in the flour, and cook for 1 minute. Add the broth, milk and seasoning and stir for 1–2 minutes, until thickened.

Unmold the loaf onto a heated serving dish, and serve the sauce separately. Garnish the dish with celery leaves.

ARMENIAN VEGETABLE STEW

SERVES 4

There are no hard and fast rules to making this Armenian specialty. It can incorporate whatever is in the refrigerator – for example, substitute turnip for carrots, cabbage for celery. It can be served as a main course or as a side dish.

Preheat the oven to 180°C/350°F. Place the oil in a large enamelled or stainless steel casserole and warm it over a medium heat. Add the garlic and stir to flavor the oil, about 2 minutes. Pour in the stock and add the bay leaf, herbs and seasoning to taste. Bring to a boil.

Add the vegetables, little by little, stirring to combine as you add them. Cover the casserole with a lid or aluminumfoil, and transfer to the oven. Bake for about 1 hour or until the vegetables are all tender, stirring occasionally.

INGREDIENTS

8 Tbsp olive oil

4 cloves garlic, crushed

I cup vegetable broth

I bay leaf

½ tsp dried tarragon

½ tsp dried oregano

salt and freshly ground black bell pepper

2 medium carrots, halved and thinly sliced

100 g/4 oz fresh stringless green beans, cut into I cm/½ inch lengths

2 small potatoes, peeled and diced

2 celery stalks, halved lengthwise and thinly sliced

I zucchini, thinly sliced into rounds

I small eggplant, halved and thinly sliced

I small red onion, thinly sliced

I small cauliflower, broken into florets

½ red bell pepper, cored, seeded and cut into strips

½ green bell pepper, cored, seeded and cut into strips

100 g/4 oz shelled fresh peas

ZUCCHINI RAGOUT

SERVES 4

This is a good way of turning zucchinis into a delicious tea-time dish or vegetarian meal. Making your own bouquet garni is important – it is better to change the herbs according to availability than to compromise with a ready-made selection.

Heat the oil in an ovenproof casserole. Add the onions, celery, carrots, garlic and bouquet garni. Stir well until sizzling, then cover and cook over medium heat for 20 minutes, stirring once.

Stir in the tomato paste and canned tomatoes with plenty of seasoning. Bring to the boil. Add the zucchini and mix well. Reduce the heat so that the mixture barely simmers, cover and cook very gently for 1 hour, stirring occasionally. The zucchini should be tender but not mushy.

Set the oven at 200°C/400°F.

Mix the breadcrumbs, cheese and parsley, then sprinkle the mixture over the zucchini . Bake for 20–30 minutes, until crisp and golden on top, then serve at once. If preferred, the topping may be broiled instead.

INGREDIENTS

3 Tbsp olive oil

2 onions, chopped

4 celery sticks, chopped

2 carrots, diced

2 garlic cloves, crushed

1 bouquet garni

4 Tbsp tomato paste

350 g/14 oz can chopped tomatoes

salt and freshly ground black pepper

650 g/1½ zucchini, peeled, seeded and thickly sliced

1 cup/8 oz fresh wholewheat breadcrumbs

2 Tbsp chopped fresh parsley

75 g/3 oz low-fat hard cheese, shredded

CREAMED CELERY SAUCE

SERVES 4

A creamy, low-fat sauce for serving with pasta – either as a topping for spaghetti or tagliatelle, or to layer with lasagne.

Trim the celery, discarding the root end and tips of the stalks. Reserve the leafy part and mince it fine (since it can be added to the sauce). Separate the stalks, scrub them, then dice each one. This is not difficult – cut them lengthwise into 3 or 4 strips, then across into dice.

Heat the oil in a large, heavy-based saucepan. Add the onion, garlic (if used), carrot, bay leaf and celery (chopped stalks and leaves). Stir well over medium heat for 5 minutes, then cover the pan and cook gently for 15 minutes to soften the vegetables.

Stir in the flour, then gradually pour in the wine and broth. Bring to a boil, reduce the heat and simmer gently, uncovered, for 20 minutes, stirring occasionally. Add seasoning to taste and stir in the low-fat cheese. Do not boil. Remove from the heat and add the tarragon or basil, then serve at once.

INGREDIENTS

1 head celery

2 Tbsp olive oil

1 onion, chopped

1 garlic clove, crushed (optional)

1 carrot, diced

1 bay leaf

3 Tbsp all-purpose flour

1 cup/200 ml/7 floz dry white wine

1 cup/200 ml/7 floz vegetable broth

salt and freshly ground black pepper

½ cup/100 g/4 oz low-fat soft cheese

1–2 Tbsp chopped fresh tarragon or a handful of basil sprigs, trimmed and shredded (optional)

INGREDIENTS

4 Tbsp olive oil

2 garlic cloves, crushed

450 g/1 lb mushrooms, sliced

1 bunch scallions, chopped

salt and freshly ground black pepper

1 bay leaf

2 x 14 oz tinned chopped tomatoes

2 Tbsp tomato paste

handful fresh basil sprigs, stalks discarded and leaves shredded

MUSHROOM AND TOMATO SAUCE

SERVES 4

Ladle this quick and easy sauce over piping hot pasta and offer freshly shredded low-fat cheese to sprinkle on top.

Heat the oil in a large pan or heavy-based saucepan. Add the garlic, mushrooms, scallions, seasoning, and bay leaf. Cook, stirring often, over medium heat for about 20 minutes, or until the mushrooms are well cooked and much of the liquid they yield has evaporated.

Add the tomatoes and stir in the tomato paste, then bring to the boil and reduce the heat. Simmer for 3 minutes, then taste for seasoning. Stir in the basil and serve the sauce.

LENTIL MOUSSAKA

SERVES 4–6

A meatless variation of the classic baked dish. This is rich, filling, and full of fiber, so it must be good for you!

Preheat the oven to 220°C/425°F. In a large pan heat 2 tablespoons of the oil. Add the onion, garlic and bell pepper and cook gently until soft. Add the lentils, red wine and tomatoes. Bring to a boil, then season and add the oregano. Simmer for 20 minutes, or until the lentils are soft. Add a little more wine to the sauce if it seems dry.

Meanwhile, heat 2–3 tablespoons of oil in a skillet. Fry the eggplant slices on both sides until tender, adding more oil if necessary, then drain on paper towels. Add any oil left in the skillet to the lentil sauce.

Heat the milk, butter and flour in a pan, stirring all the time, until boiling and thickened. Continue to cook for 1 minute, to remove the taste of flour from the sauce, then remove the pan from the heat. Add all but 2 tablespoons of the shredded cheese and then season to taste.

Layer the lentil sauce and eggplant slices in a buttered, ovenproof dish, finishing with a layer of eggplant. Spoon the sauce over the eggplants, then scatter the remaining cheese over the top. Bake in the preheated oven for 30 minutes, until the moussaka is browned and set. Serve with a salad and garlic bread.

INGREDIENTS

olive oil, for frying

1 large onion, chopped

2 garlic cloves, crushed

1 green bell pepper, cored seeded and chopped

1 cup red lentils

½ cup/110 ml/3 floz red wine

2 cups/450 g/12 lb canned chopped tomatoes

salt and freshly ground black pepper

1 Tbsp chopped fresh oregano

2 large eggplants, sliced

2½ cups/1.5 l/2½ pt milk

4 Tbsp butter, plus extra for greasing

4 Tbsp all-purpose flour

220 g/8 oz Cheddar cheese, shredded

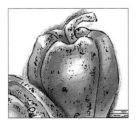

INGREDIENTS

450 g/1 lb carrots, scraped and thinly sliced

salt

200 g/7 oz can corn

1 Tbsp clear honey

½ tsp ground ginger

large pinch shredded nutmeg

3 Tbsp vegetable broth

2 Tbsp chopped fresh mint

bell pepper

oil, for brushing

Topping

4 Tbsp wholewheat breadcrumbs

1 Tbsp sesame seeds

1 Tbsp sunflower seeds

1 Tbsp wholewheat flour

5 Tbsp sunflower oil

salt and freshly ground black bell pepper

SPICED CARROTS AND CORN WITH BREADCRUMB TOPPING

SERVES 4

An unusual blend of vegetables and spices with a crunchy topping, this is a dish to prepare now and bake later.

Preheat the oven to 190°C/375°F. Steam the carrots over boiling, salted water for 8–10 minutes, until they are just tender. Mix them with the corn, honey, ginger, nutmeg, broth and mint, and season with salt and bell pepper.

Lightly brush a medium-sized oven-proof dish with oil. Spoon in the vegetable mixture, and level the top.

Mix together the breadcrumbs, seeds and flour, and gradually pour on the oil, stirring. Season the mixture with salt and bell pepper, and spread it over the vegetable layer. Bake the dish in the oven for 20 minutes until the topping is golden brown. Serve hot.

WINTER VEGETABLE CASSEROLE

SERVES 4

This recipe makes use of many winter vegetables, but use whatever you have to hand as long as there is a good mixture. Cauliflower helps to thicken the sauce slightly, therefore it is always best to include this in your recipe.

Cook the potatoes in boiling water for 10 minutes. Drain well and reserve. Meanwhile, heat 1 cup/200 ml/7 floz of the broth in a flameproof casserole dish. Add all of the vegetables, remaining broth, seasoning and paprika, and cook for 15 minutes stirring occasionally. Add the herbs and adjust the seasoning.

Lay the potato slices on top of the vegetable mixture and sprinkle the cheese on top. Cook in the oven at 190°C/375°F for 30 minutes or until the top is golden brown and the cheese has melted. Serve with a fresh, crispy salad.

INGREDIENTS

2 large potatoes, sliced

3½ pt/1.7 l/3 pt vegetable broth

2 carrots, cut into chunks

1 onion, sliced

2 garlic cloves, crushed

2 parsnips, sliced

1 leek, sliced

2 celery stalks, sliced

300 g/12 oz cauliflower florets

salt and freshly ground black bell pepper

1 tsp paprika

2 Tbsp chopped fresh mixed herbs

50 g/2 oz vegetarian cheese, shredded

VEGETABLE MEDLEY

SERVES 4

This is a delicious sauce. Serve the mixed vegetables with shells, spirals or pasta shapes rather than with long, thin pasta.

Cook the cauliflower in boiling salted water for about 3 minutes, until lightly cooked, Drain well.

Heat the olive oil and butter in a large saucepan. Add the onion, carrots and cauliflower, and stir well; then cover the pan and cook for 10 minutes. Shake the pan occasionally to prevent the vegetables sticking.

Add the zucchini, mushrooms, tarragon, lemon rind and juice. Stir well, cover the pan again, and cook for a further 2–3 minutes, or until the zucchini are bright green and tender, but with a bit of bite and full of flavor. Taste for seasoning before serving.

INGREDIENTS

150 g/6 oz cauliflower, broken into small florets

salt and freshly ground black bell pepper

2 Tbsp olive oil

2 Tbsp butter

1 onion, chopped

150 g/6 oz baby carrots, quartered lengthwise and thinly sliced

220 g/8 oz young zucchini, very lightly peeled and thinly sliced

220 g/8 oz sliced button mushrooms

1 large, leafy sprig of tarragon, chopped

shredded rind of ½ a lemon

squeeze of lemon juice

MINTED BELL PEPPER SALAD

SERVES 4

Make this cool, light, and colorful salad for a summer lunch or picnic, but do not drizzle over the olive oil until ready to serve.

Bring a saucepan of water to the boil, and add the macaroni with a dash of olive oil.

Cook for 10 minutes, until tender. Drain, rinse then place in a mixing bowl.

Mix the remaining ingredients into the pasta. Drizzle some olive oil over the salad, then serve.

INGREDIENTS

1½ cups/350 g/14 oz dried macaroni

dash of olive oil, plus extra for drizzling

1 yellow bell pepper, cored, seeded and cut into diamonds

1 green bell pepper, cored, seeded and cut into diamonds

350 g/14 oz can artichoke hearts, drained and quartered

15 cm/6 in piece of cucumber, sliced

handful of mint leaves

salt and freshly ground black bell pepper

100 g/4 oz freshly shredded Parmesan cheese

EGGPLANT WITH SPICY POTATOES

SERVES 4

Wash the eggplant. Cut it into quarters lengthwise, then, holding the pieces together, cut them across into 1 cm/½ in chunks.

Scrub the potatoes thoroughly and do not peel them, then cut each one into quarters and each quarter twice or more so that you have at least 12 bite-sized pieces from each potato.

Heat the oil in a medium-sized heavy-based saucepan and fry the onion until it turns light brown.

Add the cumin and cilantro seeds and the curry powder, if using. Fry these for a minute or so, then add the ginger, half the garlic, the chili powder, turmeric and salt. Cook this mixture over quite a high heat, adding 2 tablespoons of water as necessary so that the spice paste deepens in color and does not stick. This should not take longer than 2 minutes.

Add the eggplant, then the yogurt, and sugar. Mix everything together and cook for 2 to 3 minutes. Add 1 cup/ 200 ml/7 floz of water, lower the heat and simmer for 15 minutes, with the lid firmly on.

Add the potato, chili peppers and tomato. ensuring that the lid is firmly on, simmer for another 10 minutes, checking it occasionally to make sure that it is not sticking or burning. If it seems a bit too dry or you would prefer a little more sauce, just add a little more water and let it simmer for a few more minutes.

Lastly, add the remaining garlic, the lemon juice and cilantro leaves. Cook for 1 more minute, gently stir to mix it thoroughly and serve.

INGREDIENTS

300 g/12 oz eggplant

220 g/8 oz potatoes

2 Tbsp oil

1 sliced onion

½ tsp cumin seeds

½ tsp roasted and crushed coriander seeds

½ tsp curry powder (optional)

1 tsp shredded ginger root

4–5 cloves garlic, minced

½ tsp chili powder

¼ tsp turmeric

salt to taste

1 Tbsp low-fat plain yogurt

½ tsp sugar

1–2 green chili peppers, chopped

1 chopped tomato

1 Tbsp lemon juice

2 Tbsp chopped cilantro leaves

TOMATO SPAGHETTI WITH MUSHROOMS

SERVES 4-6

For this dish you need to include at least one kind of dried mushroom as this will give the depth of flavor that is so typical of Italian mushroom-based dishes. Dried porcini keep well, and are an ingredient that no well-stocked kitchen should be without.

Soak the porcini in warm water for about 20 minutes. Drain, reserving the soaking liquid, and chop the porcini. Heat the oil in a pan and sauté the onion and garlic for 3 minutes. Add the chopped porcini, oyster or chanterelle, and button mushrooms. Sauté for a further 5 minutes, stirring frequently.

Strain the porcini soaking liquid into the pan and add the red wine. Bring to the boil, then simmer for 5 minutes or until the mushrooms are just cooked and the liquid has been reduced by about half. Stir in the extra virgin olive oil, season to taste, and add the sage. Cover with the lid, remove from the heat, and reserve.

Meanwhile, cook the tomato spaghetti in plenty of boiling salted water for 3 to 4 minutes or until *al dente*. Drain and return to the pan. Add the mushrooms and sauce, and toss the ingredients lightly. Serve, garnished with the chopped fresh sage.

INGREDIENTS

For the sauce

15 g/½ oz dried porcini mushrooms

3 tbsp olive oil

1 red onion, peeled and cut into wedges

3–6 garlic cloves, thinly sliced

100 g/4 oz mushrooms, such as oyster or chanterelle, wiped and sliced

100 g/4 oz button mushrooms, wiped and sliced

6 Tbsp red wine

2 Tbsp extra virgin olive oil

salt and freshly ground black pepper

2 Tbsp chopped fresh sage

To serve

2 cups/450 g/1 lb fresh tomato spaghetti

chopped fresh sage

INGREDIENTS

¾ cup/150 g/6 oz thin vermicelli

2 Tbsp sunflower oil

2 lemon grass stalks, outer leaves removed and chopped

2.5 cm/1 inch piece ginger root, peeled and grated

1 red onion, cut into thin wedges

2 garlic cloves, crushed

4 red Thai chili peppers, cored seeded and sliced

1 red pepper, cored seeded and cut into matchsticks

100 g/4 oz carrot, very thinly sliced with a vegetable peeler

100 g/4 oz zucchini, trimmed and sliced with a vegetable peeler

75 g/3 oz snowpeas, trimmed and cut diagonally in half

6 scallions, trimmed and diagonally sliced

1 cup/200 g/8 oz cashew nuts

2 tbsp soy sauce

juice of 1 orange

1 tsp clear honey

1 Tbsp sesame oil

THAI NOODLES WITH CHILI PEPPERS AND VEGETABLES

SERVES 4

Rice or noodles, whether boiled or fried, form the basis of most meals in Thailand. Thai cooking is often slightly perfumed by the lemon grass which features strongly in many dishes.

Cook the noodles in lightly salted boiling water for 3 minutes. Drain, plunge into cold water, then drain again and reserve.

Heat the oil in a wok or large pan and stir-fry the lemon grass and ginger for 2 minutes. Discard the lemon grass and ginger, keeping the oil in the pan.

Add the onion, garlic and chili peppers, and stir-fry for 2 minutes. Add the red bell pepper and cook for a further 2 minutes. Add the remaining vegetables and stir-fry for 2 minutes. Then add the reserved noodles and cashew nuts with the soy sauce, orange juice and honey. Stir-fry for 1 minute. Add the sesame oil and stir-fry for 30 seconds. Serve immediately.

CHESTNUT HASH

SERVES 4

Cook the potatoes for this dish in advance or use up any leftover cooked potatoes for speed. Allow the potato to brown on the base of the pan for a crunchier texture.

Cook the potatoes in boiling water for 20 minutes or until softened. Drain well and reserve.

Meanwhile, cook the remaining ingredients in a skillet for 10 minutes, stirring. Add the drained potatoes to the skillet and cook for a further 15 minutes, stirring and pressing down with the back of a spoon. Serve immediately with bread.

3 lb/1.3 kg potatoes, peeled and diced

1 red onion, halved and sliced

100 g/4 oz snowpeas

100 g/4 oz broccoli florets

1 zucchini, sliced

1 green pepper, cored seeded and sliced

50 g/2 oz drained, canned sweetcorn

2 garlic cloves, finely chopped

1 tsp paprika

2 Tbsp chopped fresh parsley

1½ cups/300 ml/12 floz vegetable broth

½ cup/100 g/4 oz chestnuts, cooked, peeled, and quartered

freshly ground black pepper

Garnish

parsley sprigs

INGREDIENTS

100 g/4 oz green beans

150 g/6 oz potatoes

100 g/4 oz carrots

150 g/6 oz eggplant

100 g/4 oz tomatoes

1–2 green chlli peppers

2 Tbsp oil

7–8 cloves garlic, fminced

½ tsp chili powder

¼ tsp ground turmeric

½–¾ tsp salt

2–3 Tbsp fresh mint or cilantro

FIVE VEGETABLE BHAJI WITH MINT

SERVES 4

Traditionally Indian, a bhaji is a spiced vegetable dish. This one is fun because every time it is cooked it has a new taste – as the combination of the five vegetables is somehow never quite the same.

Top and tail and string the beans, then chop them into bite-size pieces.

Cut the potatoes into quarters and halve them again, preferably leaving the skin on.

Scrape and dice the carrots.

Cut the eggplant into four strips lengthwise and then slice across into 1 cm/½ in chunks.

Roughly chop the tomatoes and green chilies.

Measure the oil into a medium-sized heavy-based saucepan over a medium heat. Add the garlic, stirring it as soon as it begins to turn translucent, then add all the vegetables. Also stir in the chili powder, turmeric and salt. Mix the spices together thoroughly.

Lower the heat, cover the pan and cook for another 20–25 minutes.

Add the mint or cilantro, stir, and switch the heat off. leave to stand for 2–3 minutes before serving.

SPICY MUSHROOM OMELET

SERVES 2

Separate the eggs, keeping the whites and yolks in separate bowls and beating each.

Fold the flour into the egg yolks, together with the green or red bell pepper, mushrooms, green chilli pepper, onion and all the herbs and spices.

Mix the egg whites into the egg yolk mixture and beat once again, gradually adding 2 tablespoons of water.

Grease a large non-stick pan with the oil and heat it to smoking point.

Straight away, pour in the egg and vegetable mixture, reduce the heat and cook for 1 minute or so, shaking the pan. Then remove the pan to a hot broiler to finish cooking the omelet.

INGREDIENTS

3 large eggs

1 tsp all-purpose flour

2 Tbsp chopped green or red pepper

100 g/4 oz chopped button mushrooms

1 green chili pepper, finely chopped

1 medium onion, thinly sliced

½ tsp chili powder

¼ tsp garlic powder

1–2 Tbsp chopped cilantro

¼ tsp cumin seeds

¼ tsp salt

1 Tbsp oil

Chapter Three

Pasta

Tangy sauces and crisp
vegetables to recreate the
fiery freshness of the
Italian kitchen.

CREAMY LEEK AND PASTA FLAN

SERVES 6–8

INGREDIENTS

100 g/4 oz dried orecchiette (ears)

dash of olive oil, plus 3 tbsp

a little flour, for dredging

350 g/12 oz puff pastry, thawed if frozen

2 cloves of garlic, crushed

450 g/1 lb leeks, washed, trimmed and cut into 2.5 cm/1 in chunks

2 Tbsp chopped fresh thyme

2 eggs, beaten

150 ml/¼ pt single cream

salt and freshly ground black pepper

75 g/3 oz grated red Leicester cheese

This dish is delicious both fresh out of the oven or served chilled on a hot summer's day with a crisp green salad.

Bring a large saucepan of water to the boil and add the orecchiette with a dash of olive oil; Cook for about 10 minutes, stirring occasionally, until tender. Drain and set aside.

Dredge the work surface with a little flour and roll out the pastry. Use to line a greased, 25 cm (10in) loose-bottomed fluted flan ring. Place in the refrigerator to chill for at least 10 minutes.

Preheat the oven to 190°C/375°F. Heat the remaining olive oil in a large frying pan and sauté the garlic, leeks and thyme for about 5 minutes, stirring occasionally, until tender. Stir in the orecchiette and continue to cook for a further 2–3 minutes.

Place the beaten eggs in a mixing jug and whisk in the cream and salt and freshly ground black pepper.

Transfer the leek and pasta mixture to the pastry case, spreading out evenly. Pour over the egg and cream mixture, then sprinkle over with cheese. Bake for 30 minutes, until the mixture is firm and the pastry is crisp.

Baby Cauliflower and Broccoli Cheese

SERVES 4

INGREDIENTS

350 g/12 oz dried casareccia (long curled shapes)

dash of olive oil

50 g/2 oz butter

salt and freshly ground black pepper

6 baby cauliflowers

6 baby broccoli spears

Cheese Sauce (page 111)

3 Tbsp dry white wine

2 Tbsp heavy cream

75 g/3 oz grated mature Cheddar cheese

Baby vegetables can be both formal and fun. To make this recipe suitable for children, omit the wine and cream from the sauce.

Bring a large saucepan of water to the boil and add the casareccia with a dash of olive oil. Cook for about 10 minutes, stirring occasionally, until tender. Drain and return to the saucepan with the butter and season with salt and freshly ground black pepper. Set aside, covered, to keep warm.

Bring a large saucepan of water to the boil and add the baby cauliflower and baby broccoli. Cook for about 5 minutes, until tender. Drain and return to the saucepan, covered, to keep warm.

Place the Cheese Sauce in a saucepan and stir in the wine and cream. Heat gently, stirring constantly, for about 5 minutes.

To serve, divide the pasta between four warmed individual plates and arrange the baby vegetables on top. Pour over the Cheese Sauce and sprinkle with grated cheese. Serve immediately.

PROVENÇAL GREEN BEANS WITH PASTA
SERVES 4–6

A delicious way to serve green beans, piping hot with freshly grated Parmesan cheese.

Heat the oil in a large frying pan and sauté the garlic and onion for about 3 minutes, until softened. Add the thyme, beans, tomatoes, tomato purée, vegetable stock and wine, season with salt and freshly ground black pepper and stir well to combine. Cover and cook gently for 25–30 minutes, until the beans are tender. Remove the cover and cook for a further 5–8 minutes, stirring occasionally, until the sauce has thickened slightly.

Meanwhile, bring a large saucepan of water to the boil and add the pasta with a dash of olive oil. Cook for about 10 minutes, stirring occasionally, until tender. Drain and return to the saucepan. Toss in butter and freshly ground black pepper.

Serve the beans with the hot, buttered pasta and freshly grated Parmesan cheese.

INGREDIENTS

2 Tbsp olive oil

3 cloves of garlic, crushed

1 onion, chopped

3 Tbsp chopped fresh thyme

450 g/1 lb haricot beans, topped and tailed

400 g/14-oz can chopped tomatoes

50 g/2 oz tomato purée

1 cup/200 ml/7 floz vegetable stock

¼ cup/150 ml/¼ pt dry red wine

salt and freshly ground black pepper

450 g/1 lb dried pasta (any shapes)

25 g/1 oz butter

freshly grated Parmesan cheese

PASTA PAELLA

SERVES 6 – 8

Bring a large saucepan of water to the boil and add the farfalle with the ground turmeric and a dash of olive oil. Cook for about 10 minutes, stirring occasionally, until tender. Drain, reserving the cooking liquid, and set aside.

Heat the remaining olive oil in a large frying pan and sauté the garlic and onion for about 3 minutes, until softened. Add the red pepper, carrots and sweetcorn and stir to combine. Cook for 2–3 minutes, then stir in the mangetout, asparagus tips, black olives and farfalle. Cook for 2–3 minutes, then sprinkle the flour over and mix into the vegetable mixture. Cook for 1 minute, then gradually stir in 425 ml/¾ pt of the reserved pasta cooking liquid. Cook for 2–3 minutes, until the sauce is bubbling and thickened. Serve straight from the pan or transfer to a warmed serving dish.

INGREDIENTS

2 cups/450 g/1 lb dried farfalle (bows)

1 tsp ground turmeric

dash of olive oil, plus 3 Tbsp

2 cloves of garlic, crushed

1 Spanish onion

1 red pepper, seeded and chopped

100 g/4 oz baby carrots

100 g/4 oz baby sweetcorn

100 g/4 oz mangetout

100 g/4 oz fresh asparagus tips

75 g/3 oz black olives

15 g/½ oz plain flour

INGREDIENTS

butter, for greasing

1 cup/220 g/8 oz fresh lasagne

½ quantity Cheese Sauce (page 111)

50 g/2 oz freshly grated Parmesan cheese

For the filling

30 ml/2 Tbsp olive oil

2 cloves of garlic, crushed

1 onion, chopped

225 g/8 oz mushrooms, sliced

675 g/1½ lb frozen spinach, thawed and well drained

good pinch of freshly grated nutmeg

450 g/1 lb full-fat soft cheese

salt and freshly ground black pepper

SPINACH AND MUSHROOM LASAGNE

SERVES 6

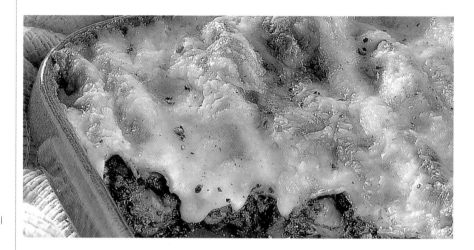

Made in advance and put in the oven before the guests arrive, this is the perfect dish for entertaining. You can relax and enjoy the company while supper sees to itself.

Make the filling first. Heat the olive oil in a large frying pan and sauté the garlic and onion for about 3 minutes. Add the mushrooms and continue to cook for about 5 minutes, stirring occasionally. Add the spinach and nutmeg and cook for about 5 minutes, then stir in the soft cheese and season with salt and freshly ground black pepper. Cook for 3–4 minutes, until the cheese has melted and blended with the spinach mixture. Preheat the oven to 200°C/400°F.

To assemble the lasagne, butter a lasagne dish and place a layer of lasagne on the bottom. Spoon some of the spinach mixture evenly over it, then add another layer of lasagne. Continue layering the pasta and spinach mixture alternately until both are used up, then pour the Cheese Sauce evenly over the top.

Sprinkle the Parmesan cheese over the lasagne and bake for about 40 minutes, until golden and bubbling.

VERDI VEGETABLES WITH VERMICELLI

SERVES 4 – 6

A lovely summer recipe to be eaten warm or cold, with chunks of crusty French bread.

Bring a large saucepan of water to the boil and add the vermicelli with a dash of olive oil. Cook for about 5 minutes, stirring occasionally, until tender. Drain and set aside.

Melt the butter in a large frying pan and sauté the sliced mangetout and the courgettes for about 5 minutes, stirring occasionally.

Add the remaining ingredients except the lime juice to the vegetable mixture and cook for a further 5 minutes, stirring occasionally. Mix in the vermicelli and cook for 2–3 minutes, until heated through. Squeeze the fresh lime juice over the mixture and serve, garnished with fresh herbs and lime slices.

INGREDIENTS

1½ cups/350 g/12 oz dried vermicelli (long, thin spaghetti)

dash of olive oil

25 g/1 oz butter

350 g/12 oz mangetout, sliced lengthways

225 g/8 oz courgettes, shredded lengthways

75 g/3 oz pimento-stuffed olives, sliced

salt and freshly ground black pepper

2 Tbsp chopped fresh parsley

2 Tbsp chopped fresh mint

squeeze of fresh lime juice

To garnish

fresh herbs

lime slices

STUFFED ZUCCHINI

SERVES 4–6

A delicious combination of tender zucchini and fresh cilantro mixed with a sweet soya sauce. You can make the filling and the sauce a day in advance. Reheat the sauce while the zucchini are baking.

Bring a large saucepan of water to the boil and add the vermicelli with a dash of olive oil. Cook for about 5 minutes, stirring occasionally, until tender. Drain and set aside.

Cut a thin slice lengthways along the top of each zucchini and chop this piece finely. Using a teaspoon, scoop out the flesh from the middle of the zucchini and chop roughly. Arrange the hollowed zucchini in a shallow ovenproof dish and set aside. Preheat the oven to 200°C/400°F.

To make the filling, place the sweet soya sauce and the garlic in a large frying pan and heat gently. Cook for about 1 minute, then stir in the mushrooms. Cook for about 5 minutes, stirring occasionally, then add the cilantro. Cook for a further 2–3 minutes, then stir in the chopped walnuts and season to taste with salt and freshly ground black pepper. Simmer for 1–2 minutes, then stir in the cooked vermicelli.

Remove from the heat and, using a teaspoon, stuff the zucchinis with the filling, placing any extra around the zucchini in the dish. Cover the dish with aluminium foil and bake for 25–30 minutes, until the zucchini are tender.

Meanwhile, to make the sauce, place all the ingredients in a food processor or blender and purée until smooth. Transfer to a small saucepan and heat gently until warm. Remove the stuffed zucchinis from the oven and serve with the cilantro sauce, garnished with finely chopped walnuts.

INGREDIENTS

½ cup/100 g/4 oz dried vermicelli (very thin spaghetti), broken into small pieces
dash of olive oil
4 medium-sized zucchini
finely chopped walnuts, to garnish

For the Filling

150 ml/¼ pt sweet soya sauce
1 clove of garlic, crushed
50 g/2 oz mushrooms, very finely chopped
3 Tbsp fresh chopped cilantro
25 g/1 oz shelled walnuts, very finely chopped
salt and freshly ground black pepper

For the Sauce

4 Tbsp olive oil
2 cloves of garlic, crushed
25 g/1 oz chopped fresh cilantro
salt and freshly ground black pepper
3 Tbsp vegetable stock

GNOCCHETTI SARDI WITH BROCCOLI AND TOMATOES

SERVES 4

INGREDIENTS

1½ lb/350 g/12 oz dried gnocchetti sardi
(small dumpling shapes)
dash of olive oil
75 g/3 oz unsalted butter
350 g/12 oz small broccoli florets
1 clove of garlic, chopped
2 tsp chopped fresh rosemary
2 tsp chopped fresh oregano
salt and freshly ground black pepper
200 g/7 oz can chopped tomatoes
1 Tbsp tomato purée
fresh herbs, to garnish

A lovely light lunch or supper dish. Choose vivid green, tightly packed heads of broccoli and cook as briefly as possible to retain the color and crisp texture.

Bring a large saucepan of water to the boil and add the gnocchetti sardi with a dash of olive oil. Cook for about 6 minutes, stirring occasionally until tender. Drain and return to the saucepan, covered, to keep warm.

Meanwhile, melt the butter in a large frying pan. Add the broccoli, garlic, rosemary and oregano and season with salt and freshly ground black pepper.

Cover and cook gently for about 5 minutes, until tender.

Add the chopped tomatoes and tomato purée and stir. Add the gnocchetti sardi, mix together lightly, then serve immediately, garnished with fresh herbs.

TOMATO AND PASTA SALAD

SERVES 6 – 8

INGREDIENTS

550 g/1¼ lb fresh orecchiette (ears)
dash of olive oil
450 g/1 lb red and yellow tomatoes,
chopped
15 cm/6 inch piece cucumber, chopped
175 g/6 oz feta cheese, chopped
5 Tbsp chopped fresh cilantro
2 Tbsp chopped fresh basil

For the Dressing

15 ml/1 Tbsp white wine vinegar
60 ml/4 Tbsp olive oil
2 cloves of garlic, crushed
salt and freshly ground black pepper

To Garnish

cherry tomatoes
fresh cilantro sprigs

Oriecchiette are small ear-shaped pasta. If they are not available, gnocchi pasta shapes (dumplings) will work just as well.

Bring a large saucepan of water to the boil and add the orecchiette with a dash of olive oil. Cook for about 5 minutes, stirring occasionally, until tender. Drain and rinse under cold running water. Drain again and set aside.

Place the orecchiette in a large mixing bowl and add the remaining salad ingredients. Mix to combine. To make the dressing, place all the ingredients in a screw-top jar and shake well. Pour the dressing over the salad and toss to coat. Serve garnished with cherry tomatoes and cilantro sprigs.

ASPARAGUS RAVIOLI WITH TOMATO SAUCE

SERVES 6

A dinner-party dish which can be made in advance – the ravioli can even be put in the freezer several weeks before the party and cooked from frozen. The sauce can be made several hours ahead and reheated before serving.

Keep the fresh pasta dough covered with clingfilm at room temperature and the Tomato Sauce in a saucepan, ready to reheat before serving.

To make the filling, heat the olive oil in a frying pan and sauté the garlic and onion for about 3 minutes, until the onion has softened. Add the chopped fresh asparagus and season with salt and freshly ground black pepper. Sauté the asparagus mixture for about 10 minutes, until softened. Set aside and allow to cool completely.

To make the ravioli, cut the pasta dough in half. Roll out one half to a rectangle slightly larger than 35 x 25 cm /14 x 10 inches. Trim the edges of the dough neatly. Cover the rectangle with the clingfilm to prevent it drying out. Roll out the other half of the dough to the same measurements. Do not trim the edges.

Place half teaspoonfuls of the filling mixture in lines, spaced about 2 cm/¾ inch) apart, all over the trimmed rectangle of pasta dough. Brush the beaten egg lightly, in lines around the filling mixture, to make the square shapes for the ravioli.

Lay the other rectangle of pasta dough on top and, starting at one end, seal in the filling by lightly pressing the dough, pushing out any trapped air and gently flattening the filling, making little packets. Using a sharp knife or pastry wheel, cut down and then across in lines around the filling to make the square ravioli shapes.

To cook the ravioli, bring a large saucepan of water to the boil and add the ravioli with a dash of olive oil. Cook for about 6 minutes, stirring occasionally, until tender. Drain and set aside.

Meanwhile, reheat the Tomato Sauce. Serve the ravioli with the Tomato Sauce, sprinkled with chopped fresh herbs.

INGREDIENTS

⅔ quantity Pasta Dough with 1 tbsp tomato purée beaten into the eggs
1 quantity Tomato Sauce
1 egg, beaten, for brushing
dash of olive oil
chopped fresh herbs, to garnish

For the Filling

30 ml/2 Tbsp olive oil
1 clove of garlic, crushed
1 onion, very finely chopped
220 g/8 oz fresh asparagus, very finely chopped
salt and freshly ground black pepper

Cheese Sauce 600 ml/1 pt

25 g/1 oz butter or margarine olive oil
25 g/1 oz flour
2 cups/600 ml/1 pt warm milk
1 tsp Dijon mustard
100 g/4 oz grated mature chedder cheese
salt and freshly ground black pepper

Tomato Sauce

As above but omit mustard and cheese and stir in 3 Tbsp tomato paste

Pasta Dough 625 g/1 ¼ lb

300 g/12 oz flour
1 tbsp salt
4 Tbsp sunflower oil
1 Tbsp water
3 eggs

CHAPTER FOUR

SALADS & SIDE DISHES

A RANGE OF TASTY EXTRAS TO
COMPLEMENT THE MAIN DISH.
ALTERNATIVELY, SELECT A
RECIPE FROM THIS SECTION TO
MAKE A DELICIOUS
LUNCHTIME SNACK.

GLAZED CARROTS WITH CILANTRO

SERVES 4

INGREDIENTS

550 g/1¼ lb carrots, scraped and cut into julienne strips

4 celery stalks, thinly sliced

juice and grated rind of ½ orange

½ cup/100 ml/3 floz vegetable stock

1 tsp coriander seeds, lightly crushed

salt and finely ground black pepper

Garnish

1 Tbsp chopped cilantro or mint

There's a special affinity between carrots and oranges – and it's not just because of their colour. This is a minus-the-fat version of glazed carrots, pepped up with ground coriander seeds.

Put the carrots, celery, orange juice and rind, stock, and coriander seeds into a pan, and season with salt and pepper. Bring to the boil and simmer uncovered over a low heat for 15 minutes or until the vegetables are tender and most of the liquid has been absorbed. Take care that the pan does not dry out. If it does, add a little more orange juice or stock.

Sprinkle with the chopped herb and serve hot.

EGGPLANT DIP WITH SUNFLOWER SEEDS

SERVES 4

INGREDIENTS

1 Tbsp sunflower seeds

50 g/2 oz grated eggplant

2–3 garlic cloves, crushed

pinch of salt

3–4 Tbsp skimmed milk

1 cup/50 g/2 oz low-fat plain yogurt

1 tsp artificial sweetener

¼ tsp cumin seeds, crushed

¼ tsp freshly ground black pepper

½ cup/25 g/1 oz chopped tomato

few mint leaves or pinch of dried mint

pinch of chili powder

Put the sunflower seeds into a heavy-bottomed skillet and heat them over a medium heat. Move the seeds around continuously with a wooden spoon, roasting them for 1 minute. Switch the heat off, but keep on stirring the seeds as the pan cools, then leave them to cool completely.

Pour ¼ cup/50 ml/2 floz of water into a small saucepan, together with the eggplant, garlic, and a pinch of salt, then bring it to a boil. Cook for 2 to 3 minutes, until the eggplant is softened to a pulp, then remove the pan from the heat and leave it to one side to cool.

Beat the milk and yogurt together in a bowl until smooth, then add the eggplant, sugar, cumin seeds, and pepper and blend well.

Add the tomato and mint leaves or dried mint.

Sprinkle the chili powder over the top and garnish with the sunflower seeds just before serving.

PINEAPPLE AND CHILI PEPPER RICE

SERVES 4

Cut the pineapple in half lengthways through the plume and scoop out the flesh. Reserve the two halves. Discard the central core, dice the remaining flesh and reserve.

Heat the oil in a pan and sauté the red bell pepper and zucchini for 5 minutes, or until softened. Add the scallions and sauté for a further minute. Stir the rice with the chili peppers, seasoning, and the reserved pineapple flesh.

Heat gently, stirring occasionally, for 5 minutes, or until hot. Then stir in the pine nuts and cilantro. Pile into the reserved pineapple shells and serve with grated low-fat cheese.

INGREDIENTS

1 large or 2 medium fresh pineapples

2 Tbsp sunflower oil

1 red bell pepper, seeded, and chopped

220 g/8 oz zucchini, trimmed and diced

6 scallion, trimmed and sliced diagonally

1 cup/250 g/10 oz cooked long-grain rice

6 jarred jalapeño chili peppers, drained and chopped

salt and freshly ground black pepper

2 Tbsp pine nuts, toasted

3 Tbsp freshly chopped cilantro

grated low-fat cheese, to serve

PAPRIKA POTATOES IN SPICY SAUCE

SERVES 6

INGREDIENTS

900 g/2 lb potatoes, scrubbed
salt
1 tsp sunflower oil
1 medium onion, chopped
1 clove garlic, crushed
1 Tbsp paprika
1¼ cup/250 ml vegetable stock
220 g/8 oz can tomatoes, chopped
½ tsp caraway seeds
1 small green bell pepper, cored, seeded, and chopped
freshly ground black pepper
3 Tbsp plain low-fat yogurt

Garnish

2 Tbsp chopped parsley

The potatoes can be pre-cooked and left in the spicy sauce, ready to be reheated while the main dish is cooking.

Cook the potatoes in boiling salted water for 5 minutes, then drain them. Unless they are very small, cut the potatoes into medium-sized slices.

Heat the oil in a saucepan, and fry the onion and garlic over medium heat for about 3 minutes, until the onion is soft. Stir in the paprika, and cook for 1 minute. Pour on the stock, and add the tomatoes (including juice), caraway seeds, and green bell pepper. Season with salt and pepper, add the potatoes, and stir well. Bring to a boil and simmer, uncovered, for 20 minutes, until the potatoes are tender and the sauce has thickened.

Stir in the yogurt, taste the sauce, and adjust the seasoning if necessary. Serve hot, sprinkled with the parsley.

MUSHROOM, PEAR, GREEN BEAN, AND WALNUT SALAD

SERVES 6

INGREDIENTS

100 g/4 oz green beans, trimmed and halved

2 ripe pears, peeled, cored, and sliced

2 tsp lemon juice

100 g/4 oz button mushrooms, trimmed, halved, or sliced

1 small bibb lettuce, washed, and drained and torn into small pieces

½ cup/100 g/4 oz walnut halves

Dressing

1 Tbsp sunflower oil

3 Tbsp plain low-fat yogurt

1 Tbsp clear honey

salt and freshly ground black pepper

This mixed fruit, vegetable, and nut salad, with its sweet-and-sour dressing, makes a substantial accompaniment to a plain dish but can also be served alone as a first course.

Cook the green beans in boiling water for 2 minutes, then drain them in a colander. Run cold water through them to prevent further cooking, then drain again.

Sprinkle the pear slices with the lemon juice, then toss them in a bowl with the beans, mushrooms, lettuce, and walnuts.

Mix the dressing ingredients, pour over the salad, and toss thoroughly. Serve.

INGREDIENTS

2 Tbsp vegetable oil

1 onion, cut in half and thinly sliced

2 dessert apples, peeled, cored, and thinly sliced

1 red cabbage, about 650 g/1½ lb, quartered, cored, and shredded

¼ cup/50 ml/2 floz red-wine vinegar

2 to 3 Tbsp light brown sugar

½ cup/100 ml/4 floz vegetable stock or water

salt and freshly ground black pepper

SWEET AND SOUR RED CABBAGE

SERVES 6

Cabbage is an important ingredient in many kitchens, especially in Russia and Central Europe. This braised sweet-and-sour cabbage dish is also delicious served cold. If you want to make the green cabbage version, use white-wine vinegar or lemon juice and white sugar.

In a large, heavy-bottomed, non-aluminium pan, over medium-high heat, heat oil. Add onion and cook until soft and golden, 5–7 minutes. Add sliced apples and cook until beginning to brown, 2–3 minutes.

Add cabbage and remaining ingredients. Simmer, covered, stirring occasionally and adding water if necessary until cabbage is tender, 30–40 minutes. Uncover and cook until liquid is absorbed. Spoon into a serving bowl.

MOROCCAN CARROT SALAD

SERVES 4

This is a favourite Middle Eastern salad, popular in Israel. It is sweet and spicy, as well as being colorful. Raw grated carrots can be used, but traditionally the carrots are cooked first.

In a food processor fitted with a grater blade, or with a hand-grater, grate carrots into a large bowl. Set aside.

In a medium skillet, over medium-low heat, heat oil. Add chopped garlic and cook until garlic begins to soften and color, 2–3 minutes. Add salt, cumin, red chili pepper flakes, cayenne or red pepper sauce, and sugar, stirring to blend.

Stir in chopped parsley and lemon juice. Slowly pour in ½ cup/100 ml/4 floz of the carrot cooking liquid. Bring to the boil and simmer 3–5 minutes. Pour over carrots. Cool to room temperature.

Cover and refrigerate 6–8 hours or overnight. Spoon into a serving bowl and garnish with parsley sprigs.

INGREDIENTS

450 g/1 lb carrots, peeled and cooked until just tender, cooking liquid reserved

2 Tbsp vegetable oil

2 garlic cloves, peeled and finely chopped

1 tsp salt

1½ tsp cumin

½ tsp red chili pepper flakes, cayenne pepper, or red pepper sauce

1 tsp sugar

2 to 3 Tbsp chopped fresh parsley

3 to 4 Tbsp lemon juice

Garnish

fresh parsley sprigs

NAVY BEANS WITH TOMATO SAUCE AND ONION

SERVES 4

INGREDIENTS

220 g/8 oz navy beans, soaked overnight, and drained

3 Tbsp virgin olive oil

3 garlic cloves, finely chopped

3 Tbsp chopped parsley

1 Tbsp chopped mixed thyme and rosemary

1 bay leaf

pinch of dried oregano

¼–½ tsp crushed red chili pepper flakes

1 cup/200 ml/7 floz water

2 large tomatoes, peeled, seeded, and diced

salt and freshly ground black pepper

¼ Spanish onion, very finely chopped

finely chopped cilantro or parsley, to serve

This recipe is distinguished from other beans in tomato sauce recipes by the addition of a mound of finely chopped raw onion and some chopped cilantro or parsley to each portion as it is served. This really livens up the dish, but it is important to use a mild onion.

Put the beans into a saucepan and just cover with water. Boil for 10 minutes and then simmer for about 50 minutes or until the beans are tender.

Heat the oil, garlic, herbs, and crushed red pepper gently for 4 minutes. Add the water, bring to the boil, then cover and simmer for 5 minutes. Stir in the tomatoes, cover again and simmer for 4 minutes.

Drain the beans and stir into the tomato mixture gently. Season and simmer for 4–5 minutes.

Ladle the beans and sauce into four warmed sup plates and put a small mound of onion and some cilantro or parsley in the centre of each.

Hot Beets in Yogurt and Mustard Sauce

SERVES 4

Ingredients

450 g/1 lb small beets, trimmed and scrubbed

salt

½ cup/100 g/4 oz low-fat yogurt

1 tsp cornstarch

2 tsp wholegrain mustard

1 clove garlic, crushed

1 Tbsp chopped mint

freshly ground black pepper

Garnish

2 scallions, trimmed and thinly sliced

A popular salad vegetable in many countries, beets have an equally attractive role to play as a hot vegetable accompaniment. This dish has middle-Eastern origins.

Cook the beets in boiling salted water for 30 minutes, or until they are tender. Drain them and, as soon as they are cool enough to handle, scrape them. If the vegetables are very small, they are best left whole; others may be sliced or diced.

Mix the yogurt with the cornstarch, and put in a pan with the mustard and garlic. Heat gently, then stir In the beets. When they have heated through, stir in the mint and season with pepper. Serve warm in a heated dish, garnished with the scallion slices.

125

JAPANESE-STYLE VEGETABLE TEMPURA

SERVES 6

Maximize the color and texture of a variety of vegetables in this crisp Japanese dish. It can be served to complement baked or broiled dishes, or presented as the main dish with brown rice.

First make the sauce. Place the ginger, soy sauce, and honey in a flameproof serving bowl, pour on the boiling water, and stir well. Leave to cool.

To make the batter, mix the dry ingredients in a bowl and gradually pour on the water, beating all the time.

Toss all the vegetables in the flour to coat them; shake off any excess. Heat the oil in a wok or deep-skillet.

Using a slotted spoon, dip the vegetables in the batter a few at a time, and allow the excess to drain back into the bowl. Fry the vegetables in several batches, reheating the oil between each one, until they are evenly golden brown.

Lift out the vegetables and toss them on crumpled paper towels to drain off excess oil. Serve at once with the sauce in a separate dish.

INGREDIENTS

Sauce

5 cm/2 in piece fresh root ginger, peeled and grated

2 Tbsp soy sauce

1 tsp clear honey

½ cup/100 ml/4 floz boiling water

Vegetables

1½ cup/300 g/12 oz cauliflower florets

2 large carrots, scraped and cut into julienne strips

1 large onion, sliced into rings

1 red bell pepper, cored, seeded, and sliced

100 g/4 oz small button mushrooms, trimmed and halved

flour, for coating

sunflower oil, for deep frying

Batter

1 scant cup whole-wheat flour

2 Tbsp fine cornmeal

2 Tbsp arrowroot

1 cup/200 ml/7 floz water

INGREDIENTS

75 g/3 oz open cap mushrooms

75 g/3 oz oyster mushrooms

75 g/3 oz shiitake mushrooms

4 Tbsp vegetable broth

2 garlic cloves, finely chopped

1 Tbsp soy sauce

1 Tbsp chopped fresh parsley or thyme

freshly ground black pepper

THREE-MUSHROOM FRY

SERVES 4

This really is a simple yet delicious dish. Three varieties of mushroom are cooked in garlic and soy sauce.

Peel the open cap mushrooms and slice thinly. Place all the mushrooms in a frying pan with the stock, garlic, soy sauce, and half of the herbs. Cook, stirring, for 3–4 minutes. Sprinkle in the remaining herbs and serve immediately.

Beet with Horseradish

SERVES 4

This flavorful side dish could also be served with blinis.

Heat the oil and stir-fry the onions for 10 minutes, until they are quite well cooked and beginning to brown. Add the beet with seasoning and continue to stir-fry for about 5 minutes for the beet to become hot, and for the flavor of the onions to mingle with it. Stir in the dill and transfer to a serving dish.

Mix the horseradish sauce with the soured cream and trickle this over the beet. Serve at once, tossing the horseradish cream with the beet and onion as the vegetables are spooned out.

INGREDIENTS

4 Tbsp oil

2 onions, halved and sliced thinly

450 g/1 lb cooked beetroot, cut in small cubes

salt and freshly ground black pepper

1 Tbsp chopped fresh dill weed

1 Tsbp horseradish sauce

½ cup/100 ml/3 floz soured cream

ZUCCHINI FRITTERS

SERVES 4

Wash and trim the zucchini. Halve them, then quarter them lengthwise.

Make a batter by beating together the eggs, cayenne, oregano and salt until well mixed.

Heat the oil in a skillet.

Dip the zucchini pieces into the batter and fry, turning once, until crisp on the outside and tender in the middle. Drain on paper towels and serve hot.

VARIATION

Eggplant, sliced ¼ in/5 mm thick, can also be cooked this way.

INGREDIENTS

450 g/1 lb young zucchini, no more than 1 in thick

2 eggs

pinch of cayenne

1 tsp dried oregano

good pinch of salt

oil for shallow frying

INGREDIENTS

350 g/12 oz precooked couscous

100 g/4 oz ready-to-eat dried apricots, sliced into strips

salt and freshly ground black pepper

1 cup/200 g/8 oz blanched almonds, lightly toasted

chopped fresh coriander, to serve

butter or olive oil, to serve (optional)

COUSCOUS WITH DRIED APRICOTS AND ALMONDS

SERVES 8

Put the couscous in a bowl and pour over 2½ cups/500 ml/1½ pt water. Leave for about 30 minutes or until most of the water has been absorbed; stir frequently with a fork to keep the grains separate. Stir the apricots and seasoning into the couscous then tip into a steamer or metal colander lined with cheesecloth. Place over a saucepan of boiling water, cover tightly with aluminum foil, and steam for about 20 minutes until hot. Stir in the almonds, coriander and butter or oil, if using.

Herbed Cauliflower

SERVES 4

Cauliflower cheese traditionally has a rich cheese sauce coating the cauliflower. This low-fat version uses a wine and herb sauce which is equally delicious.

Trim the cauliflowers and place in a large pan with the mint and stock. Cook gently for 10 minutes. Meanwhile, place the stock for the sauce, the milk, and white wine in a pan. Blend the cornstarch with 4 tablespoons of cold water and add to the pan. Bring to the boil, stirring, and add the herbs. Season and simmer for 2 to 3 minutes.

Drain the cauliflower and place in an ovenproof dish. Pour on the sauce and top with the cheese. Grill for 2 to 3 minutes until the cheese has melted. Serve immediately.

INGREDIENTS

4 baby cauliflowers

2 mint sprigs

4 cups/1 1/3¼ pt vegetable stock

50 g/2 oz cheese, shredded

For the sauce

½ cup/100 ml/4 floz vegetable broth

1½ cups/300 ml/10 floz skim milk

½ cup/100 ml/4 floz dry white wine

2 Tbsp cornstarch

1 Tbsp chopped fresh parsley

1 Tbsp chopped fresh coriander

1 Tbsp chopped fresh thyme

freshly ground black pepper

SMOKED MOZZARELLA WITH ROCKET AND WATERCRESS

SERVES 4

The piquant combination of rocket and watercress combines well with lightly smoked mozzarella in this dressing. Toss it with freshly cooked pasta shapes, such as spirals, elbows, rigatoni, penne or lumache.

Heat the oil in a small saucepan. Add the garlic, red pepper and olives. Cook for 2 minutes, then add the watercress and rocket, and stir until the leaves are just limp.

Remove the pan from the heat, and stir in the mozzarella with salt and pepper to taste. Toss into freshly cooked pasta, and serve at once.

INGREDIENTS

2 Tbsp olive oil

1 garlic clove, chopped

½ red pepper, seeded and diced

4 black olives, thinly sliced

1 bunch of watercress, leaves only, roughly chopped

6 rocket leaves, shredded

225 g/8 oz smoked mozzarella cheese, diced

salt and ground black pepper

INGREDIENTS

2 tsp cornstarch

2 Tbsp soy sauce

1 Tbsp dry sherry

2 tbsp olive oil

1 tsp sesame seed oil

1 celery stalk, cut into fine short strips

1 green bell pepper, cored seeded and cut

into fine short strips

½ onion, thinly sliced

350 g/12 oz bean sprouts

ORIENTAL BEAN SPROUTS

SERVES 4

Bean sprouts are the main ingredient for a chop suey – however, the combination of vegetables may be changed to suit the season or the contents of your refrigerator.

Blend the cornstarch with the soy sauce, sherry, and 2 tablespoons of water; set aside.

Heat both oils together, then stir-fry the celery, bell pepper, and onion for 5 minutes. The vegetables should be lightly cooked and still crunchy. Toss in the bean sprouts and stir-fry for 1 minute. Give the cornstarch mixture a stir, pour it into the pan, and bring the juices to a boil, stirring all the time. Cook for 2 minutes, stirring, then serve at once.

SAFFRON RICE AND ALMOND SALAD

SERVES 6

Put the rice, water, salt and saffron infusion in a saucepan, bring to a boil and simmer, covered, until the water has been absorbed and the rice is just tender, about 20 to 25 minutes. Take off the heat.

Combine the mustard, vinegar, oil and sugar and stir into the hot rice. Chill.

Just before serving, brown the almonds under the broiler or in a moderate oven, shaking the pan from time to time, until lightly browned. Stir into the chilled rice with the chilies, if used, and serve immediately. (If this salad is kept sitting around the almonds will lose their crunch.)

INGREDIENTS

2 cups/450 g/1 lb long-grain rice

2 ½ cups/500 ml water

good pinch salt

½ tsp saffron threads infused for

½ hour in 2 Tbsp hot water

½ tsp English mustard

1 Tbsp wine vinegar

3 Tbsp olive oil

1 tsp sugar

1 cup/200 g/4 oz blanched almonds

1–2 fresh red chilies, seeded, rinsed and thinly sliced (optional)

INGREDIENTS

350 g/14 oz fresh or frozen leaf spinach

220 g/8 oz potatoes

2 Tbsp oil

¼ tsp fenugreek seeds

½ tsp cumin seeds

1 tomato, chopped

¼ tsp turmeric

½ tsp chili powder

salt to taste

POTATOES AND SPINACH

SERVES 4

This is one of the most popular Bhajis, especially if a bunch of fresh fenugreek leaves is added to it. Use the leaves only and substitute these for 50 g/2 oz of the spinach.

If you are using fresh spinach, weigh it after you have removed the stalks and chopped it. Wash it thoroughly and leave it to drain in a colander. If you are using frozen spinach, defrost it and let it drain well in a colander.

Scrub the potatoes well and do not peel them. Cut the potatoes into quarters, then cut each quarter into 2 or more pieces, making 8 to 12 pieces from each potato. Heat the oil in a medium-sized heavy pan and fry the fenugreek and cumin seeds. As the seeds begin to sizzle, add the tomato, turmeric, chili powder, and salt. Mix and cook the mixture for half a minute. Add the spinach and potato, and mix thoroughly so that the vegetables become well coated in the spices.

Cover the pan and simmer for 15 to 20 minutes. If there is still a little moisture left after this time, remove the lid and dry it out a little by cooking rapidly over medium to high heat for another few minutes, taking care not to let it burn.

CILANTRO POTATOES

SERVES 4

INGREDIENTS

900 g/2 lb small new potatoes, scrubbed and boiled

salt and freshly ground black pepper

2 tsp superfine sugar

2 Tbsp lemon juice

4 Tbsp olive oil

3 Tbsp crushed cilantro seeds

strip of lemon

4 Tbsp snipped chives

Cilantro works wonders for new potatoes, complementing their sweet fresh flavor perfectly.

Cook the potatoes in boiling, slightly salted water for 10 to 15 minutes, or until tender. Drain. Stir the sugar and lemon juice together until the sugar dissolves completely.

Heat the oil and stir-fry the cilantro for 2 minutes. Add the lemon rind and continue to cook for a further minute, pressing the piece of rind to bring out its flavor. Tip the potatoes into the pan and then stir-fry them for about 10 minutes, or until they are just beginning to brown on the outside.

Pour the sweetened lemon juice over the potatoes and mix them well with the oil in the pan, so that the liquids mingle to form a hot dressing. Mix in the chives, check the seasoning, and serve at once.

INGREDIENTS

100 g/4 oz cauliflower

100 g/4 oz green beans

100 g/4 oz red and green bell peppers

3 Tbsp oil

3–4 whole dried chili peppers, broken roughly

1 tsp cumin seeds

¼ tsp turmeric

½ tsp salt

100 g/4 oz carrots

2 chopped tomatoes

2 tsp shredded ginger root

3–4 plump cloves garlic, chopped or crushed

1 green chili pepper, seeded andchopped

2–3 Tbsp chopped fresh cilantro

INDIAN-STYLE VEGETABLES

SERVES 4

Cut the cauliflower into small florets.

Trim the green beans and cut each one into 3–4 pieces.

Cut the red and green bell peppers into small squares.

Scrub and dice the carrots.

Heat the oil in a medium-sized heavy-based pan, then add the whole dried chilli peppers, breaking them into the pan, and the cumin seeds. As they begin to sizzle, add the turmeric and salt. Stir, then add all the vegetables, including the tomato. Mix and simmer for 2 minutes.

Add the ginger, garlic and green chili pepper and stir to blend everything together thoroughly.

Then, lower the heat, cover the pan tightly and steam cook the vegetables for 12–15 minutes.

Add the chopped cilantro and serve.

INGREDIENTS

150 g/6 oz firm white cabbage, shredded

1 small onion, minced

2 cloves garlic, crushed

1 Tbsp oil, preferably peanut

pinch of chili powder

1 cm/½ in fresh ginger, peeled and grated

2 Tbsp peanut butter

hot water

salt and sugar to taste

150 g/6 oz bean sprouts

150 g/6 oz cucumber, peeled and cubed

½ cup salted peanuts (optional)

1 fresh green chili pepper, seeded and thinly sliced (optional)

GADO-GADO

SERVES 4

Blanch the cabbage in lots of boiling salted water for 3 minutes, drain and leave to cool.

Fry the onion and garlic in the oil until lightly browned, then add the spices and fry for a minute more.

Turn down the heat and add the peanut butter and enough hot water to make the sauce a creamy consistency. Season to taste.

Combine the cooled cabbage, bean sprouts and cucumber, pour the hot sauce over them and serve at once, garnished, if you like, with the peanuts and fresh chili pepper.

PUMPKIN WITH LEEKS

SERVES 4

Stir-frying is one of the best cooking methods for pumpkin – the vegetable remains whole but slightly tender.

Heat the oil and butter until the butter melts, then add the garlic, leeks, cinnamon, and sultanas. Stir-fry the leeks for 5 minutes until they are softened and tender.

Add the pumpkin and seasoning. Continue stir-frying until the cubes are tender, but not soft enough to become mushy, which takes about 7 to 10 minutes. Serve the dish at once.

INGREDIENTS

2 Tbsp oil

knob of butter

1 garlic clove, finely chopped

2 leeks, sliced

2 tsp ground cinnamon

½ cup/100 g/4 oz sultanas

450 g/1 lb pumpkin flesh, seeded and cubed

salt and freshly ground black pepper

VEGETABLE CURRY

SERVES 4 – 6

Fry the chili peppers and garlic in the ghee or oil with the spices and lime or lemon juice for 5 minutes.

Add the onion and stir over a high heat until it begins to brown.

Add the vegetables, water and seasoning and simmer, uncovered and stirring occasionally, until the potato is cooked and most of the liquid evaporated – about 20 minutes. Serve hot.

INGREDIENTS

1–2 fresh green chili peppers, seeded and chopped

2 cloves garlic, crushed

2 Tbsp ghee or oil

1 tsp ground turmeric

1 Tbsp garam masala

1 tsp mustard seed, crushed

1 tsp ground coriander

2 Tbsp lime or lemon juice

2 medium onions, chopped

1 large potato, peeled and cubed

450 g/1 lb mixed prepared vegetables, such as: cauliflower florets; green beans, stringed and sliced; shelled peas; washed spinach, tough stems removed; etc.

2 ripe tomatoes, peeled and chopped

approx 1 cup/200 ml/7 floz water

salt, pepper and sugar to taste

INGREDIENTS

450 g/1 lb green beans, trimmed

½ cucumber, sliced thick

2 garlic cloves, finely chopped

4 mint sprigs

1 Tbsp lemon juice

½ cup/100 ml/4 floz vegetable stock

freshly ground black pepper

Garnish

strips of lemon rind

MINTED BEANS AND CUCUMBER

SERVES 4

Cucumber is not usually served hot, but it is cooked perfectly with the beans in this recipe and delicately flavored with mint. An unusual but delicious side dish.

Place the vegetables on a large sheet of aluminum foil. Bring up the sides of the foil around the vegetables and crimp to form an open package. Add the remaining ingredients, season, and seal the top of the package.

Place the package in a steamer and cook for 25 minutes or until the beans are tender. Garnish and serve.

MEXICAN TOMATO SALAD

SERVES 4

Split and seed the chili peppers and soak them in cold salted water for an hour. Rinse them and slice finely.

Peel the tomatoes. Loosen the skins by first pouring boiling water over them, letting them stand for 1 minute, then refreshing in cold water. Halve the peeled tomatoes and scoop out the seeds. Either slice the flesh or cut into chunks.

Lightly stir in the rest of the ingredients, season and chill for half an hour before serving.

VARIATION

Add 220 g/8 oz cubed or sliced mozzarella or feta cheese for a refreshing starter or a light lunch.

INGREDIENTS

1–2 fresh red chili peppers

3 large tomatoes

3–4 scallions, minced

handful fresh cilantro, minced

1 Tbsp olive oil

½ Tbsp lime juice

salt to taste

Chapter Five

Desserts

Sweet, melt-in-the-mouth desserts and puddings to round off your meal to perfection.

Ingredients

450 g/1 lb rhubarb, trimmed and cut into
2.5 cm/1 inch lengths

grated rind and juice of 1 orange

1 Tbsp water

¼ cup/50 g/2 oz pitted dates, chopped

2 Tbsp clear honey

Topping

1½ cups/ whole-wheat breadcrumbs

1 cup/100 g/4 oz rolled oats

4 Tbsp polyunsaturated margarine, melted

4 Tbsp light brown unrefined sugar

Baked Rhubarb with Oat Topping

SERVES 4

Family members who like old-fashioned puddings will love this sticky-toffee fruit layer topped with a healthful and delicious crunchy mixture.

Set the oven to 180°C/350°F. Place the rhubarb, orange juice and rind, water, dates, and honey in a 1.5 l/2 pint ovenproof dish.

For the topping, mix together the breadcrumbs, oats, margarine, and sugar, and spread the topping over the fruit. Bake in the oven for about 35 minutes, until the topping is golden. Serve piping hot.

INGREDIENTS

6 peaches

1 cinnamon stick

½ – ¾ bottle of red wine

100 g/4 oz sugar

ground cinnamon, to serve

PEACHES IN RED WINE

During the peach-growing season large bowls of these peaches are available at the Herdade de Zambujal, a huge peach-growing estate on the Costa Azul.

Preheat the oven to 180°C/350°F.

Pour boiling water over the peaches and leave for about 30-60 seconds; then remove with a slotted spoon and slip off the skins. If the skins are stubborn, return the peaches briefly to the water.

Put the peaches into a baking dish which they just fit, tuck the cinnamon stick in between them and pour over enough wine to cover them. Sprinkle over the sugar and bake for 40-50 minutes until the peaches are tender,

Remove from the oven, discard the cinnamon stick, turn the peaches over the leave to cool in the wine, turning once or twice more.

Serve dusted lightly with ground cinnamon.

MELON AND WALNUT COMPOTE

SERVES 6

Versions of this simple dessert are eaten from Greece through Georgia and Armenia to Uzbekistan.

Place the melon cubes, with any juice, in a bowl. Add the honey and toss to coat lightly. Stir in the walnuts. Divide the mixture among individual bowls.

INGREDIENTS

2 small cantaloupe or honeydew melons, halved, seeded, and cubed
1½ cups/360 ml/1⅛ pt honey
3 cups/150 g/6 oz walnuts, chopped

BLACKCURRANT SORBET

SERVES 4

INGREDIENTS

450 g/1 lb blackcurrants, fresh or frozen

4 Tbsp clear honey

⅛ cup/25 g/1 oz sugar

½ cup/120 ml/4 floz water

2 egg whites

Decoration

mint sprigs (optional)

It is reassuring to have a fruit sorbet stored in the freezer, a luxurious standby for unexpected visitors for dinner or an extra-busy occasion.

Put the blackcurrants, honey, sugar, and water into a saucepan, and bring slowly to the boil, stirring occasionally. Simmer for 15 minutes, or until the fruit is soft. Allow to cool.

Rub the fruit and juice through a sieve, and place it in a metal ice-cube tray or plastic freezer box. Cover with foil or a lid, and freeze for 1–2 hours, until the mixture is mushy and starting to set on the outside.

Beat the egg whites until stiff. Turn the fruit purée out into a chilled bowl and fold in the egg whites.

Return the mixture to the container, cover, and freeze for another 2 hours, or until firm. Stir it once or twice.

To serve, allow the sorbet to soften a little in the refrigerator for about 30 minutes. Spoon or scoop it into four individual serving glasses, and top each one with a mint sprig if you wish.

ORANGE SORBET

SERVES 6

INGREDIENTS

50 g/2 oz sugar

grated zest and juice of 1 lemon

grated zest of 3 oranges

2 cups fresh-squeezed orange juice, strained

2 egg whites, beaten to soft peaks

fresh mint leaves for garnish

Cointreau for serving

Citrus fruit sorbets and ices make an ideal dessert choice after any meal. Adding beaten egg whites gives sorbet a very smooth, creamy texture. If you prefer a rougher, 'icier' texture, omit the whites. Processing the mixture breaks up the ice crystals and contributes to a smooth texture.

In a small heavy saucepan, combine sugar, lemon and orange zests and 1 cup water. Slowly bring to the boil, stirring until sugar dissolves. Cook 5 minutes; remove from heat and cool and refrigerate 3–4 hours or overnight.

Combine lemon and orange juices with the chilled syrup and, if you like, strain for a very smooth sorbet.

If using an ice-cream machine, freeze according to manufacturer's directions.

Alternatively, put into a metal bowl and freeze 3–4 hours until semifrozen.

Into a food processor fitted with metal blade. Scrape the semifrozen mixture; process until light and creamy, 30–45 seconds. Return to the metal bowl and freeze another 1½ hours. Scrape into food processor again and process with beaten egg whites until well mixed and light and creamy, 30 seconds. Freeze 3–4 hours until completely firm.

Soften 5 minutes at room temperature before scooping into individual serving glasses. Garnish with a few mint leaves and pass the liqueur, allowing each guest to pour a little over sorbet.

YOGURT DELIGHT

SERVES 4

Mix the yogurt, orange zest, and 2–3 tbsp of the honey, then divide it between four dishes and chill well.

Melt the butter, then stir fry the pistachios and Brazils with the raisins for 3 minutes. Add the pears and continue to stir fry for about 3 minutes, or until the pears are lightly cooked. Stir in the apricots and orange juice and bring to the boil. Boil, stirring, for 2 minutes to reduce the orange juice.

Stir in the grapes and remaining honey (or to taste) and heat through briefly. Spoon the fruit and nut mixture on top of the chilled yogurt and serve at once.

INGREDIENTS

3 cups/150 g/6 oz low-fat yogurt

grated zest and juice of 1 orange

¼–½ cup/60-120 ml/2-4 floz clear honey

knob of unsalted butter

½ cup/25 g/1 oz shelled pistachio nuts

½ cup/25 g/1 oz Brazil nuts, roughly chopped

½ cup/25 g/1 oz raisins

2 firm pears, peeled, cored and diced

¾ cup/40 g/1½ oz ready-to-eat dried apricots, sliced

½ cup/25 g/1 oz seedless grapes, halved

DAIRY MOLDS

SERVES 6

A delicious low-fat version of the French *coeur à la crème*, this dairy blend makes a light and delightful accompaniment to berries of all kinds.

Strain the cottage cheese into a bowl. Beat in the yogurt.

Pour the water into a small bowl, sprinkle on the gelatin, stir well, and stand the bowl in a pan of warm water. Leave for about 5 minutes for the gelatine to dissolve. Pour the gelatin mixture into the cheese and beat well.

Spoon the cheese into 6 individual molds. Heart-shaped ones are traditional, or you can improvise by using ramekin dishes or yogurt tubs covered with cheesecloth and inverted. Stand the molds on a wire rack over a plate and leave them to drain in the refrigerator overnight.

Turn out the molds, and serve well chilled.

INGREDIENTS

2 cups/220 g/8 oz low-fat cottage cheese

½ cups/100 g/4 oz plain low-fat yogurt

3 Tbsp warm water

1 Tbsp powdered gelatin

INGREDIENTS

1 ogen or canteloupe melon, seeded and
sliced in thin wedges and peeled
3 sweet seedless oranges, peeled and
segmented, juice reserved
1 mango, peeled and thinly sliced
24 fresh lychees, peeled, or 1 450 g/16 oz
can lychees in their own juice
12 Medjool dates, cut in half lengthwise and
pitted
1 pomegranate, cut in half, seeds reserved
(optional)

Garnish

fresh mint leaves

SLICED EXOTIC FRUITS WITH DATES

SERVES 6

Fruit salad has always been a popular dessert and almost any seasonal fruits are delicious sliced or cut up together in their natural juices or with a fruit purée. This is not a traditional fruit salad, but a selection of exotic fruits, sliced and served together. Ogen melons from Israel are as sweet as sugar, as are the Israeli oranges. California produces a wonderful variety of date, the Medjool date, which is recommended for this dish.

Arrange slices of melon on each of six individual plates in a fan shape. Arrange peeled orange segments and mango slices in an attractive pattern over the melon slices.

Evenly distribute fresh or canned lychees over fruit and sprinkle on some reserved fruits from all fruits.

Arrange four date halves on each plate and sprinkle with the pomegranate seeds, if using. Garnish with fresh mint leaves and serve.

Ingredients

75 g/3 oz rolled oats

5 Tbsp Scotch whisky

3 Tbsp clear honey

1 cup/ low-fat cottage cheese, sieved

1½ cups/220g/8 oz plain low-fat yogurt

1 tsp grated orange rind

220 g/8 oz blackberries, hulled

Decoration

fresh mint

BLACKBERRY AND WHISKY OATIE

SERVES 4

Put the oats and whisky into a bowl, cover, and set aside for at least 2 hours, or overnight if it is more convenient.

Beat together the honey, cheese and yogurt and stir in the orange rind. Stir in most of the blackberries.

In four tall glass dessert dishes, make layers of the fruit mixture and oats, beginning and ending with the fruit. Decorate each glass with a few reserved berries and a sprig of fresh mint. Serve chilled.

Iced Blackcurrant Soufflé

SERVES 6

Always select plump juicy fruit.

Wrap a double thickness of aluminum foil around a soufflé dish to extend 5 cm/ 2 inches above the rim of the dish. Cook the blackcurrants with the superfine sugar until soft, purée in a blender, and then strain. Allow to cool. Whisk the egg whites until stiff, then gradually whisk in the confectiner's sugar.

Whip the cream until softly stiff. Place the fruit purée in a large bowl and gradually fold in the egg white and cream. Pour into the prepared soufflé dish, level the surface, and freeze for several hours until solid. Remove the foil and serve.

INGREDIENTS

650 g/1 ½ lb blackcurrants, hulled

½ cup/100 g/4 oz sugar

2 egg whites

1 cup/200 g/8 oz confectioner's sugar, sifted

1 ¼ cups/300 ml/½ pt whipping cream

BLUEBERRY CHEESECAKE

SERVES 6

Line the base of an 20 cm/8 inch springform cake tin.

Place the muesli and dried figs in a food processor and blend together for 30 seconds. Press into the base of and chill while preparing the filling.

In a saucepan, sprinkle the gelatine onto 4 tablespoons of cold water. Stir until dissolved and heat to boiling point. Boil for 2 minutes, then cool.

Place the milk, egg, sugar and cheese in a food processor and blend until smooth. Stir in the blueberries. Place in a mixing bowl and gradually stir in the dissolved gelatine. Pour the mixture onto the base and chill for 2 hours until set.

Remove the cheesecake from the tinand arrange the fruit for the topping in alternate rings on top. Drizzle the honey over the fruit and serve.

INGREDIENTS

For the base

1 cup/220g/8 oz natural granola

100 g/4 oz dried figs

For the filling

1 tsp vegetarian gelatine

⅔ cup/150 ml/¼ pt skim evaporated milk

1 egg

½ cup/100 g/4 oz fine granulated sugar

2 cups/220 g/8 oz low-fat cottage cheese

300 g/12 oz blueberries

For the topping

100 g/4 oz blueberries

2 nectarines, pitted and sliced

2 Tbsp clear honey

INGREDIENTS

For the mousse

1¼ cup/325 g/10 oz low-fat plain yogurt

1 cup/100 g/4 oz skimmed milk cheese or cream cheese

1 tsp vanilla essence

4 Tbsp vanilla sugar

1 Tbsp brandy or sherry

2 tsp vegetarian gelatine

2 large egg whites

For the sauce

350 g/14 oz raspberries

juice of 1 orange

½ cup/100 g/4 oz confectioner's sugar, sifted

VANILLA MOUSSE

SERVES 4

This light and fluffy mousse tastes as good as it looks. It is sliced and served with a delicious raspberry sauce.

Place the yogurt, cheese, vanilla essence, sugar and alcohol in a food processor, blend for 30 seconds until smooth. Pour into a mixing bowl.

Sprinkle the vegetarian gelatine onto 4 tablespoons of cold water in the saucepan. Stir until dissolved and heat to boiling point. Boil for 2 minutes.

Cool, then stir into the yogurt mixture. Whisk the egg whites until peaking and fold into the mousse.

Line a 3½ cup/1.7 l loaf pan with plastic wrap. Pour the mousse into the prepared pan and chill for 2 hours until set. Meanwhile, place the sauce ingredients in a food processor and blend until smooth. Press through a strainer to discard the seeds. Unmold the mousse onto a plate, remove the plastic wrap, pour a little sauce onto a plate, slice the mousse, and serve.

STRAWBERRY TERRINE

SERVES 8

Ripe strawberries in a liqueur-flavored jelly make a spectacular centerpiece for a dinner party or buffet table. You can substitute other berries, or carry the idea into another season and use orange sections instead.

Put the sugar, orange rind and water into a pan and bring slowly to the boil, stirring occasionally. Boil for 5 minutes, then remove from the heat and allow to cool a little. Sprinkle on the gelatine crystals and stir well. Set aside to cool, but do not allow to set. Strain the syrup into a jug through a fine mesh strainer lined with paper towel, and stir in the liqueur or brandy.

Rinse a 2 pint/1.2 l mold with cold water, and arrange the quartered strawberries to make a pattern. Slowly pour the syrup over the fruit, taking care not to displace the fruit. Cover the mold with aluminum foil and place it in the refrigerator for several hours or overnight.

Unmold the terrine, run a hot knife between the gelatine and the mold and place a cloth rinsed in hot water over the base for no more than a few seconds. Place a serving plate over the mold, quickly invert the plate and the mold together, and shake sharply to release the dessert.

Decorate the dessert with fresh strawberries. You can hull the fruit if you wish, but it looks more decorative and provides a natural element of contrast if you do not.

INGREDIENTS

1½ cups/325 g/10 oz superfine sugar
thinly-grated rind of 1 orange
2½ cups/500 ml/12 floz water
4 Tbsp (4 envelopes) powdered gelatine
2 Tbsp kirsch or brandy
2¼ lb/1.2 kg fresh strawberries, hulled and quartered

Decoration

220 g/8 oz strawberries, halved

INGREDIENTS

220 g/8 oz seedless red grapes

4 egg yolks

3 Tbsp superfine sugar

4 Tbsp Marsala, Madeira or sweet sherry

GRAPE CUSTARD

SERVES 4

This delightful dessert is so quick and simple to make. It is ideal for a dinner party.

Wash the grapes and place in the bottom of four individual glasses.

Place the egg yolks in a bowl. Beat lightly, add the sugar and wine, and mix together. Place the bowl over a pan of hot water and whisk until the mixture is thick and creamy. This could take about 10 minutes.

Divide the mixture among the glasses and serve at once while still warm with sponge fingers.

APRICOT PRALINE PAVLOVA

SERVES 6

A spectacular dessert to draw delighted comments at the end of a special meal, and proof that pavlova, a filled meringue basket, does not have to be filled with whipped cream.

Soak the apricots in the orange juice for at least 2 hours, or overnight; place in a saucepan, bring to the boil, and simmer for 20 minutes until the fruit is tender. Allow to cool, then purée the apricots and any remaining juice in a blender or food processor and beat in the yogurt.

To make the praline, put the honey and caster sugar into a small pan and bring to the boil. Boil for 5 minutes, until very thick. Remove from the heat, and stir in the almonds. Pour into an greased pan, and leave to cool.

Set the oven to 140°C/275°F. To make the meringue, whisk the egg whites until they are very stiff. Fold in half the granulated sugar, and whisk again until the mixture is stiff and glossy. Fold in the remaining sugar.

Line a baking sheet with waxed paper, and spoon the meringue to make a nest. Bake in the oven for 1 hour, or until the meringue is firm. Leave it to cool, then peel off the paper, and place it on a serving dish.

Coarsely crush the praline with a rolling pin or in the blender. Just before serving, spoon the apricot mixture into the center of the meringue, and sprinkle on the praline.

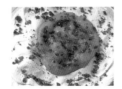

INGREDIENTS

220 g/8 oz dried apricot pieces

1¼ cup/250 ml/10 floz orange juice

¾ cup/175 ml/5 oz plain low-fat yogurt

Praline

6 Tbsp set honey

2 Tbsp superfine sugar

1 cup/220 g/8 oz chopped blanched almonds

oil, for brushing

Meringue

3 egg whites

1 cup/220 g/8 oz granulated sugar

I N D E X